WHAT TO SAY
AND HOW TO SAY IT
TO YOUR TEEN

Books by Tim Shoemaker

*The Very Best, Hands-On, Kinda Dangerous
Family Devotions*, vols. 1–3

WHAT TO SAY
AND HOW TO SAY IT
TO YOUR TEEN

A PARENT'S GUIDE TO **30** TRICKY CONVERSATIONS

TIM SHOEMAKER
AND MARK SHOEMAKER

a division of Baker Publishing Group
Grand Rapids, Michigan

© 2025 by Tim Shoemaker and Mark Shoemaker

Published by Revell
a division of Baker Publishing Group
Grand Rapids, Michigan
RevellBooks.com

All rights reserved. No part of this publication may be reproduced, stored in a retrieval system, or transmitted in any form or by any means—for example, electronic, photocopy, recording—without the prior written permission of the publisher. The only exception is brief quotations in printed reviews.

Library of Congress Cataloging-in-Publication Data
Names: Shoemaker, Tim, author. | Shoemaker, Mark, author.
Title: What to say and how to say it to your teen : a parent's guide to 30 tricky conversations / Tim Shoemaker and Mark Shoemaker.
Description: Grand Rapids, Michigan : Revell, a division of Baker Publishing Group, [2025] | Includes bibliographical references.
Identifiers: LCCN 2024060807 | ISBN 9780800747190 (paperback) | ISBN 9780800747527 (casebound) | ISBN 9781493451555 (ebook)
Subjects: LCSH: Parenting—Religious aspects—Christianity | Parent and teenager—Religious aspects—Christianity | Teenagers—Religious life.
Classification: LCC BV4529 .S433 2025 | DDC 248.8/45—dc23/eng/20250313
LC record available at https://lccn.loc.gov/2024060807

Unless otherwise indicated, Scripture quotations are from the Holy Bible, New International Version®, NIV®. Copyright © 1973, 1978, 1984, 2011 by Biblica, Inc.® Used by permission of Zondervan. All rights reserved worldwide. www.zondervan.com. The "NIV" and "New International Version" are trademarks registered in the United States Patent and Trademark Office by Biblica, Inc.®

Scripture quotations labeled ESV are from The Holy Bible, English Standard Version® (ESV®). Copyright © 2001 by Crossway, a publishing ministry of Good News Publishers. Used by permission. All rights reserved. ESV Text Edition: 2016

Scripture quotations labeled NIV1984 are from the Holy Bible, New International Version®, NIV®. Copyright © 1973, 1978, 1984 by Biblica, Inc.® Used by permission of Zondervan. All rights reserved worldwide. www.zondervan.com. The "NIV" and "New International Version" are trademarks registered in the United States Patent and Trademark Office by Biblica, Inc.®

This publication is intended to provide helpful and informative material on the subjects addressed. Readers should consult their personal health professionals before adopting any of the suggestions in this book or drawing inferences from it. The author and publisher expressly disclaim responsibility for any adverse effects arising from the use or application of the information contained in this book.

Cover design by Chris Kuhatschek

Appendixes B and C are taken from Tim Shoemaker, *The Very Best, Hands-On, Kinda Dangerous Family Devotions*, vol. 1, copyright © 2019. Used by permission of Revell, a division of Baker Publishing Group.

The authors are represented by the literary agency of Cyle Young Literary Elite, LLC.

Baker Publishing Group publications use paper produced from sustainable forestry practices and postconsumer waste whenever possible.

25 26 27 28 29 30 31   7 6 5 4 3 2 1

To our better halves, Cheryl and Sarah.
Parenting—and ministry—is a partnership.
Without the insights, patience, encouragement,
and godly input from our wives,
this book probably wouldn't have happened.

CONTENTS

Preface   11

Introduction: *The Conversation That Changed My Life*   13

PART 1 Setting Ourselves Up for Good Conversations with Our Teens

1. Prepping for the Talk with Your Teen   19
2. Good Timing   25
3. What Not to Say   30
4. You'll Need More Than Two Ears When Listening to Your Teen   35
5. Handling Their Objections   39
6. Five Things You Need to Know About the Next Part of This Book   42

PART 2 Scenarios for Thirty Important Talks with Our Teens

7. Family   47
   Lack of Respect for Mom or Dad   47
   Your Teen Fights or Argues with Siblings Too Much   51

8. Phones and Screen Time 56

*Your Teen Wants Their Phone in Their Bedroom
   at Night 56*
You Realize the Need to Limit Screen Time 60
Warning Teens Before They Get Involved in Porn 65
You Suspect or Know Your Teen Is into Porn 70

9. Friends or Dating 76

*Asking to Stay Overnight at a Friend's—
   but You Don't Approve 76*
*You're Not Comfortable with the Friends Your
   Teen Chooses 80*
*Your Teen Thinks They're Ready to Date—
   but You Don't 85*
Your Teen Wants to Date a Non-Christian 89

10. Their Walk with God 96

Your Teen Doesn't Want to Go to Church 96
Your Teen Questions If You Have the Right Religion 102
Your Teen Is Questioning the Truth of God's Word 107
*Your Teen Wonders How God Can Allow Bad Things
   to Happen 112*
*Concerns Your Teen Isn't Growing in Their Faith/Spending
   Time in the Word 116*
*Concerns Your Teen Isn't Being Kind, Loving,
   or Demonstrating Fruit of the Spirit 121*

11. Personal Habits and Behavior 126

Being Responsible and Productive with Their Free Time 126
Texting Versus Real Conversations 130
Your Teen Is Using Language You Don't Approve Of 134
*Preparing Them for Their First Job—with Better
   Work Habits 139*
You Want Them to Get a Job 145

You're Seeing Pride Issues   150
You're Seeing Anger Issues   154
Teen Dishonesty   158
Concerns About Demonstrating Good Leadership   162

12. **Their Emotions**   168

   Your Teen Seems to Be Depressed   168
   Your Teen Seems Consumed with Anxiety   173
   Your Teen's Self-Worth Seems at an Unhealthy Low   180

13. **Their Personal Views and Conforming to Culture**   186

   Your Teen Is Developing Views That No Longer Agree with Scripture   186
   Helping Your Teen Navigate Truth About Identity and Gender   190

Appendix A: *Strategies to Make It Easier for Teens to Accept What You're Saying*   199

Appendix B: *Watch Your Step Family Activity*   207

Appendix C: *Easy Target Family Activity*   213

PREFACE

> For I did not speak of my own accord, but the Father who sent me commanded me **what to say and how to say it.**
>
> John 12:49 NIV1984

Jesus didn't just say whatever popped into his head. He deliberately made sure the things he said were in tune with God the Father, so he'd know ***what to say*** and ***how to say it.*** If Jesus was that careful, it makes sense that we follow his lead.

In *What to Say and How to Say It to Your Teen*, Mark and I (Tim) share insights on how parents can more effectively handle different scenarios that come up with teens—or conversations that *need* to happen. We'll give some input based on our own experiences, sure. But more importantly, we'll be looking to Scripture, because what parents say and how we say it to our teens matters to God.

Are you ready? Let's do this!

—Tim and Mark

INTRODUCTION

The Conversation That Changed My Life

I (Tim) had messed up. Bad. It was the worst thing I'd done in my teenage life up until that point. It wasn't just that I'd made an honest mistake. I'd deliberately sinned. I'd thought I could get away with it—but I hadn't figured on how strong conviction can be.

In a late-night confession, I finally admitted to my mom what I'd done. We agreed we'd talk again the following night when Dad was there.

All that next day, I dreaded the coming conversation. The three of us sat around the kitchen table, and at first everyone was dead quiet. My siblings had been exiled to the basement.

Honestly, I don't remember one thing I said. But I do know how my dad opened the conversation. His face was an emotional mix of pain and frustration. Mostly pain.

"I don't know what to do with you, Tim. I don't know if I should hit you or what."

Hit me. Hit me, I silently begged him. I deserved it. Maybe if he hit me hard enough, I could get my mind off what I'd done.

Dad didn't hit me; he didn't yell. He didn't threaten me. He didn't put me down or treat me like I was stupid. Just the opposite, in fact. He affirmed how smart I was. How responsible. How proud he was of the decisions I usually made. Which is why my sin shocked him so much, I think. He knew that wasn't who I wanted to be. Maybe he also knew how deep my regret had cut into my soul. I get choked up just remembering that night.

My parents didn't ground me. They didn't punish me—although I wouldn't have blamed them if they did. But clearly, I'd broken trust with them and grieved them. And that was far worse than any punishment I could imagine.

They forgave me. And it wasn't just empty words. They backed it up with action. There were things that had to be done as a result of my sin. Things to take care of. My dad did those things *with* me. He had to drive me someplace to get part of it done. He never mentioned my sin while we were in the car. Never rubbed my nose in it. My parents never told the rest of the family how I'd messed up. And they didn't hold it over my head by bringing it up again. Not once. Not ever. I'm still in awe of that.

Dad and Mom's reaction to me didn't give me any reason to rebel against them. In fact, the way they talked to me in that moment of my confession—and in the days that followed—was one of a handful of life-changing events for me. Clearly, they allowed God to work through them, which absolutely paved the way for God to do a deeper work in me. I never wanted to grieve or disappoint my parents like that again. I worked at that. And I worked hard to build back their trust.

Our teenagers are going to mess up. They're going to break trust. They're going to hurt us. And how we react at those times is critical. Do it well, and we nudge them toward true repentance. Do it not so well, and we push them deeper into rebellion.

That's why this book was written, and why a team of people contributed to it behind the scenes in their unique ways. This book is about giving parents some tools to help keep our teenagers on—or get them *back* on—the right paths. Don't skip the next six chapters: "Prepping for Your Talk with Your Teen," "Good Timing," "What Not to Say," "You'll Need More Than Two Ears When Listening to Your Teen," "Handling Their Objections," and "Five Things You Need to Know About the Next Part of This Book." These chapters provide important tips to give you an edge—and reminders you'll need over and over. And you'll find a gold mine in appendix A, "Strategies to Make It Easier for Teens to Accept What You're Saying."

I want to encourage you to have the conversations in this book with your teen. The forces of darkness strategize to mess up our sons and daughters. We need to help protect our kids from the clutches of a very evil and brilliant enemy. Often that means we must reset our priorities, putting our needs aside to help our kids through this time. Let's do that. We don't have much time. Just a few short years. Maybe less. And with God's help, we *can* do it. By God's grace, my wife and I have three sons who didn't rebel against us or God in their teen years. It can be done . . . one conversation at a time.

After my parents talked with me that night, I'm pretty sure my dad went to bed feeling exhausted—and like a failure. But he'd won a major victory. He just didn't know it. With God's help, he'd spoken right to my heart, and I was changed as a result.

As parents we often feel like failures. But take heart, my friend. God has a way of turning those moments into major victories.

PART 1

SETTING OURSELVES UP for GOOD CONVERSATIONS with OUR TEENS

PREPPING FOR THE TALK WITH YOUR TEEN

I (Tim) scuba dive, and every time I do, I have a goal. Explore a reef. A wreck. See the marine life. Recover something that had been lost. Find one of those massive prehistoric shark teeth. It varies with each dive. But my goal, whatever it is, is always *secondary* to my primary objective. And that primary objective never changes. It's the same for each dive . . . every single one:

RETURN SAFELY, BOTH ME AND MY DIVE BUDDY.

If I push my secondary goal into the primary spot, the chances of disaster happening increase. I may compromise. I may stretch my time on the bottom a bit too long. Go deeper into a wreck than I can safely go. I may not stay as close to my buddy as I should.

It's the same during conversations with our teens. Sure, we'd love to bring them around to our way of thinking or see them have a change of heart. But those are *secondary* goals.

My primary objective for every talk with our son or daughter: *Return safely, both me and my teen.* If we as parents let our secondary goal overshadow the primary, the likelihood of our conversation with our teens going bad skyrockets. We'll push too hard. Too long. We'll be more desperate and less patient. But returning safely means that at the end of the conversation, we aren't further from our teens than when we started talking. Ideally, we're closer to them and our understanding of each other is a little bit better.

How do we return safely? We prep for the talk.

Here are four ways to prep. Likely there are more that will work best for you—and you can add them. But this needs to be easy to remember, so let's go with an acronym: PRAY.

1. **Pray.** Pray that you'll say the right things. That your teen will hear you. That you'll hear your teen. That God will give you the words and the insight. That this conversation would draw you and your teen closer, not push you further apart.
2. **Reinforcements.** Enlist the help of another prayer warrior when you can. Your spouse. Maybe Grandma or Grandpa. A mentor. One or two is enough.
3. **Atmosphere.** Where will you have this talk? How can the place you choose help keep the conversation from going south? (We'll get back to this in a minute.)
4. **Your objectives.** What are the primary and secondary objectives you want to accomplish with this talk? (We'll circle back to this point as well.)

Atmosphere Is Important

We should always pick a place where interruptions are limited, so, obviously, we'll put away our phones while we're talking—and our teens will too. But sometimes there's more we can do. Our teens want to be seen as adults, right? And we want our teens to act like adults. See the common denominator here? You and your teenager both want this to be an adult thing. Where do adults have adult conversations? Often they meet at a restaurant. If we're planning a big, important conversation, sometimes taking our teens to a restaurant is really smart. We'll be showing our teens respect and giving their concerns or well-being our full attention.

At a restaurant, the conversation is also a bit more likely to go better. There's a whole lot less chance of our teens shouting or pouting. They probably won't stomp away from the table—like they may at home. That opens the door for a more productive conversation. And when the talk is over, your teen can't disappear to their room. You'll still have time together to help reinforce your love for them over dessert, or on the drive home.

Restaurants aren't always the answer, though. A face-to-face conversation—for more than a couple of minutes—can be hard for teens. It's uncomfortable. They're less likely to open up when they feel we're looking at them the whole time. They'll feel like they're under the microscope. They'll look down a lot. They'll avoid eye contact. And if we tell them to look at us, that would be a mistake. We're putting them in a straitjacket, and they'll likely give us dead or very resentful eyes.

We'll often have better conversations with our teens if they're someplace where they don't have to look us in the eye—and they know we aren't staring at them. That's why good conversations are easier when we take them for a drive. We're looking out the windshield, with only occasional glances their way. They're looking out the windows themselves.

Another good option? Take a walk. Our teens won't feel like we're staring at them, so they'll open up easier. Shooting hoops works too. They're able to be active, which helps with nervous energy, and they don't have to look us in the eyes.

One of the best places to have a talk with a teen is in a darkened room, such as their bedroom—or ours—at night. They can't see our faces, and they know we can't see theirs. Perfect. Often a mom will sit on the side of the bed. If it would be natural for her to rub her teen's back or stroke their arm as they talk, Mom will gain another advantage. She'll feel her teen tense at points in the conversation, and she'll probably be able to read them as if they were talking in daylight.

Personally, I'll choose a dark room or a drive almost every time—at least when it comes to my own kids. I may not see their face, but I can hear their tone. Their pauses or hesitations. They all mean something. We'll have the Holy Spirit helping us discern what's really going on too, right?

Another thought: If we're having this conversation at home, on a drive, or during a walk, it's often smart to pick up some kind of snack, treat, or something to drink. Eating or drinking gives our teens something to do with their hands, which is helpful during talks they find uncomfortable. In the Bible, what was Peter feeling after he'd denied Christ? Massive discouragement and guilt, for sure. Enough to make him quit the ministry and go back to fishing. Jesus met him on that beach . . . and gave him something to eat. Immediately after that, Jesus got Peter to express some of his deepest feelings. We need every advantage we can get when talking with our teens. To me, that's a good enough reason to pick up something for my son or daughter to eat while we talk.

Objectives

Whatever we're hoping to accomplish with the talk is secondary. Remember the scuba diving analogy—and how that must influence our conversation. The primary objective for every conversation never changes: *Return safely, both me and my teen.*

Sticking to that can be tough to do in the moment. Especially if a teen is rebelling or has made a mess in some way. To help ensure the conversation hits this primary objective, here are some reminders to review before a big conversation:

- *Remember how much you love your teen.* Sure, they can be hard to live with at times. So, before that conversation, think about them the way they used to be. When they were younger. When seeing you made them beam. That child is still in there. How will you show them you love them—even if you're disappointed in them or upset with them? How will you show them you care? Because you really do. You love your teen, so don't let your worries about the conversation cloud your face. Smile.
- *Remind yourself you're not going to argue.* No matter what. Consider Philippians 2:14–15:

    > Do everything without grumbling or arguing, so that you may become blameless and pure, "children of God without fault in a warped and crooked generation."

- *Remind yourself to be kind in tone and in what you actually say. Show love in those ways.* Set your intensity dial at the right level. Is this issue as big of a deal as you're making it? How might you feel about this issue or conversation five years from now? How do you want your teen to look back on the conversation someday? Be a thermostat. Set the temperature for the tone of the talk. This is a good time to remember 1 Corinthians 16:13–14:

    > Be on your guard; stand firm in the faith; be courageous; be strong. Do everything in love.

    This is so critical. And remember, according to 1 Corinthians 13:1, if you aren't speaking in love, all your teen will hear is irritating noise. You won't get through to them.
- *Don't exasperate your teen. Don't push their buttons. Don't insult them.* Resolve not to drop into the cheap

tactics we'll cover in chapter 3, "What Not to Say." Review that list before every big talk with your teen, and remember Ephesians 6:4:

> Fathers, do not exasperate your children; instead, bring them up in the training and instruction of the Lord.

Sometimes you'll want to use alternate strategies to get through to your teen more effectively. There are times when trying something a bit more creative works better than simply sitting down and having a conversation with your teen. Every scenario in this book includes a referral to appendix A, "Strategies to Make It Easier for Teens to Accept What You're Saying," to give you at least one other alternate idea of how to approach the topic.

Using a strategic object lesson is one alternate strategy to potentially make some conversations easier. The object lessons we'll suggest are found in the three-volume set *The Very Best, Hands-On, Kinda Dangerous Family Devotions*. These books will prove to be a great tool. Buy the set now so you have it on hand when you need it (see appendix A for more information). If an alternate approach outlined in those books makes just one conversation easier or more effective, they're totally worth it. Jesus taught us the power of using visuals, object lessons, and stories to teach. Sometimes the best way to make a point with your teen is through a demonstration or activity. These books also work great as a way to teach your teen important life lessons on a regular basis.

Mom, Dad, we want to encourage you. Put in the effort to prep for these talks with your teen. Sometimes that extra time makes all the difference. Remember, there's an enemy who wants to derail our kids. We want to do everything we can to keep that from happening.

2

GOOD TIMING

Timing is everything. Well, maybe not *everything*, but when we're having a conversation with our teens, timing is massively important.

Sure, there are times when the timing stinks but delaying isn't an option. In those cases, we pray for the best and simply start the conversation. But we must make sure that we're not just impulsively jumping into the talk because *we* want to deal with it right now.

We all know the story of Jesus turning over the tables in the temple.

> On reaching Jerusalem, Jesus entered the temple courts and began driving out those who were buying and selling there. He overturned the tables of the money changers and the benches of those selling doves, and would not allow anyone to carry merchandise through the temple courts. And as he taught them, he said, "Is it not written: 'My house will be called a house of prayer for all nations'? But you have made it 'a den of robbers.'" (Mark 11:15–17)

But jump back four verses earlier.

> Jesus entered Jerusalem and went into the temple courts. He looked around at everything, but since it was already late, he went out to Bethany with the Twelve. (v. 11)

When Jesus overturned the tables, he didn't lose his temper and go on a rampage. Jesus was completely in control. The night before, he'd seen there was a problem that absolutely needed to be addressed. But the timing wasn't good. It was late. Jesus delayed the confrontation until the following day. We're wise to take this to heart. Jesus demonstrated the importance of timing. Sometimes we need to be patient. We must focus on getting the best results, not getting something off our chest. And often that means we need to take time to pray, think through the situation, and prep before we speak. We're wise to also consider a teen's schedule when it comes to the timing of the conversation. Check out Proverbs 27:14: "If anyone loudly blesses their neighbor early in the morning, it will be taken as a curse."

Blessing your neighbor by complimenting them or building them up in some way is a good thing. But doing it so early in the morning that we rob them of desperately needed sleep? *Not* good. We can have great intentions, and may even say good things to our teens, but if our timing is bad, it'll blow up in our face.

Telling our teens that we love them to the moon and back? Great. But choosing bad timing—like telling them in front of their school friends? Ugh. Or worse yet, writing that message on posterboard and holding it up in the stands while they're playing with their team? They'll want to send *you* to the moon.

When we talk to our teens, let's pick the timing carefully. If we decide to have a serious talk with them while their friends are waiting outside, we can't expect great results. If we turn off the movie they're watching or the game they're playing to have our little heart-to-heart, we're off to a bad start. Our teens will interpret that as us having no consideration for them.

Choose a time that won't compete with something they already have planned or are busy doing. Sometimes the best time might be after they're in bed. We're not taking them from something they really want to do. Other times we might want to invite them to hop in the car. We can take them to a favorite fast-food place, buy them a shake and fries, and have our talk.

Be creative. Give the issue of timing some thought. Conversations with our teens can be hard enough without throwing bad timing into the mix. Let's be wise and choose our timing carefully.

What if there's no time to prepare? Sometimes a tough conversation gets set in motion without warning—or time for prep. Even if we feel we have no choice but to have the conversation at that time, there's always one thing we can do. *Must* do. And there are a few quick things we must remember.

One Thing We Must Do

The one thing we must do is shoot up a quick prayer. We can learn from Nehemiah, an Israelite living as an exile in a foreign land after the nation of Judah had been defeated. He served as a cupbearer to the conquering pagan king. Nehemiah had heard a report of how Jerusalem was in ruins, and the news grieved him. He prayed God would do something. King Artaxerxes noticed the change in Nehemiah and asked what was troubling him. Nehemiah did something that serves as an example of what to do when any of us are cornered into a conversation without a chance to fully prepare.

> In the month of Nisan in the twentieth year of King Artaxerxes, when wine was brought for him, I took the wine and gave it to the king. I had not been sad in his presence before, so the king asked me, "Why does your face look so sad when you are not ill? This can be nothing but sadness of heart."

I was very much afraid, but I said to the king, "May the king live forever! Why should my face not look sad when the city where my ancestors are buried lies in ruins, and its gates have been destroyed by fire?"

The king said to me, "What is it you want?"

Then I prayed to the God of heaven, and I answered the king. (Neh. 2:1–5)

Nehemiah was afraid, but he breathed a silent prayer on the fly. Likely he asked God to guide his words—and the king's reaction. There wasn't time to ask for more. That's exactly what we do when we're thrust into a serious or potentially scary conversation without adequate time to prep. We pray. It's something quick.

A Few Things to Remember

If we feel this is a really bad time for the conversation, and we can tactfully delay it just a bit to allow for some prep time (or so that our spouse can join us), we should go for it. *But we can't stall indefinitely.* Preferably we'll handle it that same day, or the next. Let's set the time. Lock it in.

Here are three examples of things we might say to delay that conversation without offending our teens.

- "I'm glad you brought that up. We really do need to talk about this. How about we do this: Let's set this up for (give a time). I don't want to jump into this too quickly. There's a couple of things I need to think through before we talk. Will that work for you?"
- "I'm glad you brought that up. We really do need to talk about this. How about we do this: Let's set this up for (give a time) so Dad/Mom can join the conversation too. Will that work?"
- "I'm glad you brought that up. We really do need to talk about this. How about we do it where/when we can talk

with less interruptions? I want to give you my full attention. Let's do it at (give a time) when your little brother is in bed. Does that work for you?"

If our teens are agreeable to the delay, we must be sure we have a time locked in. Next, we get busy with our prep. Remember the acronym from chapter 1: PRAY.

3

WHAT NOT TO SAY

Having conversations with our teenagers about important issues can be really, really tough. It's easy for our teens to misunderstand us and often hard for them to see the big picture behind our intentions. Next thing we know, the conversation takes a bad turn. Our teens get defensive—or go silent and sullen. So, we want to be smart. We want to do everything we can to keep the conversation good and effective. We know our teens. Their weak areas. Their vulnerable points. We know where their buttons are, and it would be easy to push them. But that would be a form of exasperating our kids, which violates a clear command God gives parents in Ephesians 6:4:

> Fathers, do not exasperate your children; instead, bring them up in the training and instruction of the Lord.

What does exasperating our kids look like?

- Belittling our teens in any way, including talking down to them.
- Using sarcasm when talking to them.

- Accusing them—especially if we claim to know their motives when only God does.
- Interrupting them without asking for permission first.
- Acting annoyed or impatient with them as they talk.
- Arguing or debating them as they try to explain themselves.
- Laughing at them. This is especially lethal.
- Making fun of them, mocking them, or embarrassing them in any way.
- Using classic manipulating or controlling tactics, like guilting them into doing what we want them to do.
- Finishing their statements rather than giving them the time to collect their thoughts.
- Failing to hear them out, even though we're absolutely sure we know where they're going with their conversation. Pressing ahead without letting them finish, even if they're repeating themselves, will sabotage the conversation. As Proverbs 18:13 says, "To answer before listening—that is folly and shame."
- Intimidating. Threatening. Using fear instead of love to get them in line.

These are bully tactics—every single one. If we exasperate our kids, we're following the enemy, not the Lord. We're playing into the enemy's hand, and he uses *us* as a weapon against our kids. That's messed up. Let's not make our enemy's job easy. We should speak the truth, but only in love.

Conversation Killers

Here are some specific "conversation killers," things we want to avoid saying when talking with our kids—no matter how much we may feel like it.

"When I was your age . . ."

Here's the sad truth: For the most part, they don't care about our life as a teenager. Chances are our teens already think they're sooo different from us. And they see the world of our teenage years as being completely different from their world. A comparison of our teenage years to theirs only widens the chasm between us. Someday they may be interested in our childhood. But let's give them ten or twenty years on that.

"Someday, when you have your own home, you can live any way you want. But while you live under my roof, you'll do it my way."

Okay, it is very tempting to say this—and our enemy hopes we do. We might as well pour gasoline onto the bridge connecting us to our teens and toss a match. We're the adults, and we've got to be more together than to use an inflammatory, belittling statement like this one.

"I don't care what you want/think."

But we absolutely *do* care what our teens think, right? We'd do anything to rewind the clock somehow, to go back to when they adored us. A comment like this will absolutely push them further away.

Also, this comment is a lie. We don't want our teens lying to us, so we shouldn't lie to them. Usually, we say something like this when we're emotionally frustrated. If we use a lame-o line like this, we're only reinforcing what our teens honestly believe deep down: that we don't care. They're convinced we're coming down on them because we're only concerned about what's best for us—not what's best for them. Think about that. We've got to show them a different side of us.

"You always . . ." or "You never . . ."

That's not completely true, is it? When we don't acknowledge that our teens do get it right *sometimes*, that gives them less incentive to get it right *ever*.

"I don't care what your friend's parents let them do."

We'd *better* care. These are the friends who may have more influence on our teenagers than we do. What kind of freedoms do their parents give them? We'll want to know; it will help us better prepare for how we'll handle issues with our teens.

"The Bible says . . . !"

Now, of course we want to use the Word. It's the source of truth. It's also a massively powerful tool. We're careful with power tools, aren't we? They come with safety guards, switches, and sensors so we don't hurt ourselves—or anyone else. We need that same perspective with the Word. We don't want to use Bible verses as a club to beat our teens down or into line. They'll rebel against that eventually. We must be very careful of our tone when we bring Scripture into the discussion. We want to win their heart, not simply the argument. Of course we'll want to use Scripture. But we'll want to use it to show God's love for us—and how he knows and wants what's best for us.

"You'll do what I say because I said so / because I'm the parent/boss."

Okay, these tired lines have been used for generations. Maybe your mom or dad said it to you, and your grandparents said it to them. But statements like these aren't going to lead us to anything good. They may be true, but they're bully talk. Seriously: This is parental bullying.

And nobody thinks that what a bully does is good or right or fair. If we make statements like these, here's what our teens hear: *"I'm more powerful than you—and I hold all the cards. You'll do it my way or else."*

And if that's what our teenagers hear, they'll daydream about the day when they're stronger than us, and how they'll put us in our place. We don't want that.

I've seen many parents use these types of conversation killers—and sometimes they got positive results. But only *temporarily*. Those parents only got behavior changes with their teens, not heart changes. It always comes back to haunt those parents eventually. If we make a habit of using any of the above tactics, our relationship with our teens often changes, leaving us much worse off than we ever imagined. Our bridges to our teens will burn, and we'll be stranded and unable to reach them.

Instead, we want to help our teens grow into the kind of people God intended them to be. That will be easier to do if we avoid saying the things on this list.

If you have teenagers, you may only have a couple of years left with them living under your roof. You want those years to be good. You want to finish strong. If you do that, you can be sure they'll be coming to you for advice and counsel as they get older. And someday when *they* have kids, they'll trust Grandma and Grandpa to babysit, something you'll desperately want.

Bridges are easy to destroy but hard to rebuild.

4

YOU'LL NEED MORE THAN TWO EARS WHEN LISTENING TO YOUR TEEN

When our kids were little, we could get away with multitasking. They could babble, and we'd just add our "mm-hmm" now and then while most of our focus went to whatever task we were doing.

But as our kids got older, that changed—or it should've. Unless we make obvious efforts to pay attention when they talk, our teens will accuse us of not listening. In conversations that matter to our teens, they're likely watching us closely. We want to make sure they see us caring enough about them to listen well.

Here are a few essential things we can practice when in important conversations. None of this stuff should be a surprise, but it never hurts to review the list. We need our teens to truly believe they're being heard if our conversation is going to achieve any lasting good. And hey, the truth is, we need every tool and trick we've got to figure out what our teens are—and are *not*—saying.

- **Pray.** Before. During. Ask for the right tone, patience, insight, wisdom, and so forth.
- **Look their way.** Obviously, we can't do this constantly if we're driving, for example. But we want to watch their body language for all those nonverbal clues as to what they're thinking. How are they reacting to what we're saying?
- **Beware of anything distracting in our line of sight.** A TV screen in a restaurant begs us to look at it, even if the volume is down. If we go to a restaurant for our talk, we can't turn off their TV, but we can sit at an angle where we don't see it.
- **Put away the phone.** Seriously. Switching it to silent mode isn't enough. If that thing buzzes in our pocket, we'll be distracted.
- **Be aware of our facial expressions.** Sometimes, when we concentrate, our expression can almost look angry. Watch for that. What does your intensely concentrated face look like? If you don't know, go find a mirror right now. Or set your camera up for a selfie and take an honest look. Since I (Tim) know what my concentrated face looks like, I make efforts to change that during conversations.
- **Be aware of body language.** Arms crossed. Hands on hips. Neither of these communicates that we're listening with an open mind. Sometimes a nod is good. It shows we agree with them—or at least we get what they're saying.
- **Demonstrate we've got all the time in the world, even if we don't.** Try not to look at a clock, watch, or phone. We have to watch that we don't tap our foot or do anything that can be interpreted as being impatient. We can deliberately take a pretty relaxed position if seated, like at a booth in a restaurant. Maybe we kick back and put both legs up

on the bench seat. We want them to get the message that we've got all the time they need.

- **Take notes when appropriate.** Plan on taking notes, especially if the conversation is over the phone. We don't use these notes to cross-examine our teens or anything but rather to help us remember. And often when we're reviewing our notes, we'll make some connections that help us—which helps them.

- **Resist the urge to interrupt, even if they've got something clearly wrong.** Instead, circle back later, after they're done, if appropriate. The only exception would be to ask questions about things we're unclear on, and not in a challenging way but purely for clarification. We hold up a hand first—and ask permission. "One second . . . can you clarify something you just said?" *And after they explain, remember they still have the floor.* This isn't the time for us to comment on those things.

- **When they're done giving their side of things, we repeat what we've heard back to them, as needed, to be sure we're understanding them.** This is another good reason to jot some notes during the conversation. It demonstrates a sincere desire to understand them.

- **Now we share our point of view.** We want to be careful not to give off a vibe that says, "Okay, I listened to you—now you need to listen to me." And as we share, let's be careful. Concise. If we gush out all our feelings, they'll feel like they're being emotionally waterboarded. Maybe, through this process, a solution is obvious to us. We can toss it out there. Or better yet, we can invite our teens into the problem-solving process. "Okay, you've made some really valid points. So, let's put our heads together on this. There's got to be a solution we can both be okay with."

- **Do all we can to make sure the conversation ends on a good note.** We don't want to leave the table with tension still in the air.
- **When at a restaurant, plan to tip extra—and let the server know.** We don't want a server to keep coming back with the "Is there anything else I can get you?" line that makes us feel they want to turn over the table. That could nudge a conversation to end early. Right up front, we can let the server (and our teens) know we might be there awhile, but that we'll tip accordingly.

You'll add to this list, I'm sure. And if we *really* want to know how to listen better and to look like we're giving our teens our full attention, we'll get input from others. A mate. Our own parent. Someone we know who seems to parent well. The point is, we need every advantage we can get if we hope to understand our teens—and get them to open up. We need two ears. Two eyes. We need to be aware of how we look to our teens. And we definitely need the Holy Spirit to give us insight and wisdom.

5

HANDLING THEIR OBJECTIONS

"But you don't understand!"
"You never listen!"
"This isn't fair!"
"What's the point of talking to you? You always . . ."

If our teens make one of these statements, we need to realize they truly believe we're not listening. Maybe it's our tone. Our body language. It may even be the things we're saying.

If they don't believe they're being heard, they truly feel they're being given a raw deal. It may be immature on their part, but we have to meet them where they're at. That's what Jesus did, right?

It's hard. We may know exactly where our teens are going with their argument. We may want to move on. Get to the point. We want to fix this and get it over with. The temptation is to cut them short and save a little time.

But if we hear one of these statements, we should realize our teens don't feel they have a voice. They believe the fix is in—and that our mind is made up without hearing them out. That's fertile ground for growing anger and resentment. No matter how unfair we think our teens are being or how dead wrong we know they are, when we hear them say something like this, we've got to change our tactics—or risk massive damage.

Let's be sure we're really following those good listening practices covered in the previous chapter and take a moment to review a few things that become critically important if our teens don't believe we're hearing them.

1. **If we're multitasking in the slightest way, we must stop.** That might be part of the problem.
2. **Pray again.** Quick. Silent. Desperate.
3. **Further reduce distractions.** We've already turned off the phone/TV. Did we miss anything?
4. **Double our efforts to show we want to hear them out.** If it looks like we're waiting to pounce—champing at the bit to say our piece—we'll be doing damage. This is about entering their world and learning whatever we can. We don't want a strained relationship with our kids. That's agonizing. So, we listen, even when we don't feel we have the time. And as we do, we're looking for clues as to what they're thinking and how we might resolve this.
5. **Reinforce our love for our teens during and after tough conversations.** Our love is a whole lot deeper than whatever issue putting us at sword points with each other.

If our teens don't believe we're truly listening to them, they'll find someone else who will. Often that person *isn't* someone who will back us up—or share our views. Scary thought, right?

Now, even after we've completely heard them out, it may not change the course of action we believe we have to take. And our teens won't be happy with that news. But it will be a whole lot worse if they don't feel we've actually made an effort to hear them.

Another objection we might encounter here is more of a stalling technique: "Don't you trust me?" If our teens hit us with this kind of response, we have to recognize it for what it is. *Manipulation*. Maybe not 100 percent of the time, but often a statement like this is made by a person seeking to control the conversation or the outcome.

To assure them of our complete trust is pointless. They make the statement not because they want assurances of our trust but to get us to do what they want us to do. Perhaps the issue is no phones in our teens' bedrooms at night—and they give the "Don't you trust me?" line.

We might handle that objection with something like this:

"I probably trust you more than you think. And I want to trust you even more—which will come in time if this goes well.

But I'll tell you who I don't trust. The enemy. I don't trust him enough to leave you vulnerable at night. I've seen how the enemy uses a phone at night to rob teens of sleep, impair their judgment, increase their anxiety, bully them, add more opportunities for temptation, and more."

Mom, Dad, in each of the scenarios we tackle throughout this book, we'll have a section called "When to Follow Up." Most conversations we have will require us to circle back with our teens—even when the talk goes well. When a tough conversation is over, there's no way we'll want to step into that arena again, but we need to. Especially if they've had objections. You can do this, my friend. Our God can help.

FIVE THINGS YOU NEED TO KNOW ABOUT THE NEXT PART OF THIS BOOK

There are thirty scenarios to come in part 2 of this book. Here are five things you need to know about them before diving in.

1. **You don't need to stay in the order of the table of contents.**

    In many cases, you'll want to tackle an issue as it comes up in your family—or as a practical way to disciple your kids. You might put a date in the margin of the *Table of Contents* to note when you talked to your teen about it and a date for when you followed up.

2. **You'll likely want to cover each scenario with your teen at some point.**

    Even if you don't think it's an issue with your teen, we want to encourage you to talk with your teen about it. It may become an issue for them in the future—without you realizing it. Or they may have a friend who is struggling, and you'll be equipping your teen to help.

3. **Each scenario is broken into the same five sections.**

   Why This Is Important. This gets down to the heart of the issue. You'll be strengthened to have the conversation . . . because you'll really see what's at stake.

   What to Say. This is where you'll find suggestions as to how to open the conversation and cover the important points. And remember, it's okay to have notes with you when you talk to your teen. It's also fine to put things in your own words.

   Alternate Way to Say This. Sometimes a traditional conversation with your teen may not be the only—or the most effective—way to handle the issue. With each scenario we'll make suggestions for an alternate method or two.

   When to Say This. Timing is important . . . and we'll give our best suggestions as to when to have the conversation.

   When to Follow Up. We'll make suggestions here because every one of the conversations needs follow-up. In fact, you really haven't finished the conversation about the issue until you follow up.

4. **You don't have to wait until they're teenagers.**

   Many if not all of these scenarios cover issues you can talk to your kids about much earlier. In many cases, it'll be easier to do so because your kids are still listening to you. And by talking about these things earlier, your kids will be protected sooner.

5. **Review the first five chapters in part 1, "Setting Ourselves Up for Good Conversations with Our Teens."**

It's so easy to forget some of those basics about listening, body language, handling objections, the different elements of the PRAY acronym, and more. A quick skim will set you up for better conversations—with less conflict.

PART 2

SCENARIOS for THIRTY IMPORTANT TALKS with OUR TEENS

7

FAMILY

LACK OF RESPECT FOR MOM OR DAD

Eye rolls. Heavy sighs. Sarcasm. Scowling stare downs. Rudeness. Isolating themselves. Disobedience. Arguing. Embarrassing us in public. Teens have a full arsenal of ways to show their lack of respect for their parents. The kids who once adored us seem barely able to tolerate us. Many parents take one of two courses of action. Unfortunately, both lead to the same place: failure, loss, and regret.

- *The "tough love" approach.* They play the tough parent, demanding respect—or else. It comes across as a whole lot more "tough" than loving. I (Tim) have never seen this approach work over the long haul. Not once. This strategy might change things temporarily on the surface, but rarely will it change a teen's heart. All they're doing is hiding their true feelings—for now.
- *The "wait this out" approach.* This is about enduring the disrespect. Parents following this path clutch a pie-in-the-sky hope that a change will just somehow happen—or long for the day their teen moves out.

A better approach? *Love them enough to confront them in a caring way.* I know . . . we're tired. But it's the only course of action that I've found to work. And when it does, the payoff is absolutely life-giving.

Why This Is Important

If our teens continue down this road of disrespect, what might happen to *them*? Here are three reasons we need to put in the effort to deal with this kind of disrespect—right away.

- *Because it's important to God.* He made it part of the Ten Commandments.

   > Honor your father and your mother, as the LORD your God has commanded you, so that you may live long and that it may go well with you. (Deut. 5:16)

- *Because it's important for our teens' well-being.* The verse above says that life will go better for our teens if they honor and respect their parents. That's a promise from God. See also Ephesians 6:1–3. If our teens continue on this road of disrespect toward us, can we really expect they'll receive God's best blessings? We know better. And if they don't respect us, they won't come to us for advice. So, they'll make more poor choices—some with life-crippling consequences. Clearly, if they're not respecting us, life will be harder for them. This is high-stakes stuff.
- *Because it's important for our health—physical and emotional.* Parents of disrespectful teens pay a massive price. As Proverbs 17:25 says,

   > A foolish son brings grief to his father
   >   and bitterness to the mother who bore him.

WHAT TO SAY

Can you think of a time recently when your teen showed proper or exemplary respect for someone? Mention that incident . . . and how proud that made you feel as a parent. Now mention the concerns you have.

"Sometimes I'm really concerned with how you disrespect Mom or Dad. It's easy to do because we're not perfect. And I'm sure lots of your friends talk about times they're frustrated with their parents. But I think you're so much bigger than that."

Before you go any further, remember to control your tone. The more "parental" your voice sounds to them, the more resistance you'll get.

And remember this truth: *It's really hard to rebel against someone we totally respect.* If your teen is disrespecting you as a parent, you can guess you lost their respect, maybe in the distant past, and you'll need to get to the bottom of that.

"So, the thought occurred to me that I said something or did something—or failed to say or do something—that caused you to lose respect for me. Do you remember what that was?"

This is hard. Sooo hard. If they open up, you'll need to pray for God's help not to defend yourself. Even if you think they're being utterly unfair, resist the urge to argue—or they'll clam up for good.

Ask the Lord to help you find a road back. It starts with asking him for forgiveness for how you've failed and then asking your son or daughter for forgiveness.

Now you can help your teen understand why this issue of respecting parents is so important. It's for their good. I'd go right to Ephesians 6:1–3:

> Children, obey your parents in the Lord, for this is right. "Honor your father and mother"—which is the first commandment with a promise—"so that it may go well with you and that you may enjoy long life on the earth."

Remember, you're not beating them over the head with this. You're pleading with them and trying to win back their heart. The fact is, if they're failing to show respect or honor to their parents, they've set themselves in opposition to Almighty God. Who is likely to win that matchup?

Alternate Way to Say This

Check out the object lesson/activity "Watch Your Step" in appendix B. This makes a great alternative.

If your teen won't say what's causing them to disrespect you, another alternate approach might be to bring in help. See the Handoff or Ask the Expert approach in appendix A.

When to Say This

The biggest danger comes from stalling this conversation, putting it off while waiting for the "right day." I'm begging you . . . don't. Disrespecting parents is a form of gangrene in the lives of our teens—and family. The longer we let it go untreated, the bigger the loss. If there is a root of disrespect, whatever is inside them will grow stronger by the day.

Taking them out to eat in a public place often increases the likelihood that they'll be more civil, which will make the conversation a bit easier on everyone.

When to Follow Up

After you've had that initial talk with them, circle back no more than a week later. Before you do, be sure you have the right heart and the right attitude.

If your teen *did* open up and reveal why they lack respect for you, you need to be working hard to change. When you follow up with your teen, this is where you start. You might ask them how *you're* doing. Are your changes moving in the right direction? Remember, if they've lost respect, it will take *time* to rebuild it. In this follow-up conversation, you're just looking to be sure you're heading in the right direction.

Next, you can talk to them about how *they're* doing. Was there a moment when you saw some improvement? Comment on that. Urge them to keep going. Remember, you're not looking simply for behavior change but for a real softening of the heart.

This loss of respect as a parent is incredibly tough. Keep going. Think of Galatians 6:1:

> Brothers and sisters, if someone is caught in a sin, you who live by the Spirit should restore that person gently.

Often, we think of using this verse for people in the church, but it can apply to our teens, too, especially when they're caught in the trap of disrespect.

YOUR TEEN FIGHTS OR ARGUES WITH SIBLINGS TOO MUCH

Wishing your kids simply got along with their siblings and never became irritated or upset with each other? Pretty unrealistic. But that doesn't mean you settle for a Wild West home environment, either. No parent wants to continually play the sheriff, breaking up fights and enforcing the peace.

Why This Is Important

As parents, we're to:

- *Provide* for our kids.
- *Protect* our kids.

- *Prepare* our kids for the future.
- Be *present* for our kids . . . to be there for them and to be Exhibit A as to what being a Christian is all about.

Helping our kids survive and thrive in an environment where people irritate them and don't always share their opinions is a massive part of preparing them for their future. If our teens learn these things now, they'll do better in many areas of life.

WHAT TO SAY

It's easy to simply issue orders.

- Stop arguing/fighting.
- Don't speak to your brother/sister that way.
- Be kind.
- Talk nice.

You may not always have time to do more than play the sheriff and, in essence, order the kids to holster their weapons. But that won't help your teen in the long run.

Sometimes it helps to open this conversation in a more active way. You might pick up a metal pot lid or pie pan and a spoon. Drum on that metal lid/pan with that spoon—loudly—while reading 1 Corinthians 13:1 to your teen in a normal or quiet voice.

"If I speak in the tongues of men or of angels, but do not have love, I am only a resounding gong or a clanging cymbal."

Okay, you can stop hitting the metal now.

"It was kind of hard to hear what I was saying while I was hitting that, right? This verse illustrates a life truth. No matter how appropriate or true the words coming out of our mouth are, if they don't come from a heart of love, they're just an annoying noise to the person we're talking to."

Give them a moment to process that, then bring this closer to home.

"Sometimes when I hear you fight or argue with your brother/sister, I feel neither of you are talking in a loving way. You're both just making noise—and accomplishing nothing good or helpful. But there's another way to look at the situation when you and your brother/sister are having differences."

Here are some things you'll want to cover, in your own words.

- God puts us in families with a variety of personalities for our benefit. It's a way to prepare us to be successful throughout our entire lives—in a world of people who think very differently than we do at times.
- When we're upset or irritated or frustrated with someone, saying whatever pops into our head is often dangerous, destructive, and not at all what God wants us to do.
- Those moments when we get irritated and our anger flares up or we get exasperated with someone are part of our spiritual training ground. These times teach us to ask God to help us respond in truth and kindness and love.
- The better we get at this, the more our home will be a safe place to be—and one where we'll feel happier and more supported ourselves.
- The better we get at this, the better our friendships will be, too, and the more we'll be appreciated and will do well in our job or occupation someday.
- Someday you'll likely be married to someone you love with all your heart. But if you don't learn now—in the family God has placed you in—how to speak with love when you're irritated or angry or frustrated, you'll hurt that mate you love, too, and sometimes those wounds won't easily heal.

Give your teen a moment to digest this, then share God's standard from Scripture.

> Do not let any unwholesome talk come out of your mouths, but only what is helpful for building others up according to their needs, that it may benefit those who listen. And do not grieve the Holy Spirit of God, with whom you were sealed for the day of redemption. Get rid of all bitterness, rage and anger, brawling and slander, along with every form of malice. Be kind and compassionate to one another, forgiving each other, just as in Christ God forgave you. (Eph. 4:29–32)

"Can you imagine how good life would be if we really lived that way? If we consistently surrendered to God to become that kind of person?" Consider making it a challenge for each member of the family to be more aware of how they talk and to work at speaking in love over the next week.

Alternate Way to Say This

This is a topic you'll need to hit more than once—and a variety of methods help. The Game/Challenge approach as described in appendix A is a simple way to make a game out of this. If everyone goes a week without arguing or fighting, what kind of family prize might you offer at the end? Another way to talk about this? The Object Lesson approach offers plenty of creative ways to highlight how families talk to each other, or check out "Take a Stab at Kindness" in *The Very Best, Hands-On, Kinda Dangerous Family Devotions*, vol. 1.

When to Say This

Pick a time when everyone is calm. If you're upset at that very moment with how your teen is talking, you'll come on too strong or forceful. And if you've just broken up an argument, they may be too worked up to listen. They're still thinking of some scathing things to say to their sibling.

When to Follow Up

Follow up a week after your initial conversation. You want to encourage them along if you saw any examples where they did it right.

One last thought: Our teens often reflect how *we're* doing with this issue.

- Do we get sarcastic or snippy with our spouse?
- Are our words harsh or rude?
- Do we belittle others or get critical?
- Do we speak in love—or are we just making noise?

Let's pay attention to the example we're giving; our kids will be watching—and listening too.

PHONES AND SCREEN TIME

YOUR TEEN WANTS THEIR PHONE IN THEIR BEDROOM AT NIGHT

There's an old saying that warns against letting a camel stick its nose under your tent. Soon the whole camel will be in your tent, leaving little space for you. What starts small and seemingly harmless turns into a big problem!

If we've allowed our teens to keep their phones in their bedrooms at night, likely we've learned just how real that camel analogy can be. Parents often find they have less and less space in their teen's life.

The problem is, our teens *love* this camel. So, keeping that phone out of their room—or removing that privilege—is going to be really, really tricky.

Why This Is Important

There are so, so many reasons this is important. Here's a few.

- *Sleep.* We don't need a survey to tell us that phones cause our teens to lose massively needed sleep at night. If a teen is awake just one hour extra a night due to their phone, they lose an entire night of sleep every week. Phones add to the already rampant sleep deprivation problem.
- *Attitude.* With less sleep comes more problems. Anxiety. Crabbiness. Sibling tensions. Arguing with Mom or Dad.
- *Capability.* As sleep deprivation increases, capabilities decline. Do you want your teen's ability to make good decisions going down? What about their grades? What do they miss because they're tired all day? Might it impact their driving ability?
- *Protection.* Cyberbullying. Predators. Sexting. Porn. Screen addiction. All of these are very real and can happen while you're sleeping soundly. Letting teens keep a phone in their room is like putting a lockless door in their bedroom that allows them to sneak out of the house at night—or allows strangers in.

WHAT TO SAY

This conversation is monumentally easier if these two things are in place:

- First, you've set a good example of phone use yourself, especially at night.
- Second, you've set the policy of "no phones in bedrooms at night" long before you gave your teen a phone. If they want a phone—and they do—they'll agree to your terms. Setting up the house rule of no phones in

bedrooms at night is fairly easy. Just never, *ever*, let that camel put its nose in the tent. Once you allow an exception to the rule, a lot more exceptions will come up.

Now, if your teen *has* been allowed to keep their phone in their room all night, you know you need to change that. Before talking to your teen, remind yourself that you have every right to regulate their phone use.

- Who bought the phone? You did.
- Who pays for the phone plan? Odds are you do that too.
- Who must give account to God for how you raise and protect your kids? Ah, yes . . . that would be you again.

Taking your teen out to eat for this conversation can work well. In a restaurant, they may behave better than if you brought this up at the kitchen table. When the time is right, start the conversation.

"Have you ever said or done something that you realized later was a huge mistake?"

Be prepared to give a personal example, especially if they don't have one. Then move on to the issue at hand.

"I've made lots of mistakes like that. Some I could go back and fix, others not so much. But once I know I've made a mistake, I can't keep going in that direction. Does that make sense?"

They may not answer, but likely they're tracking perfectly.

"And there's a mistake I made that I need to fix. It involves you. You may not like it. And if I didn't love you as much as I do, maybe I'd just keep going this way. I know this is going to be a tough one for you; that's why I've been praying about this conversation. I'm praying that you'll understand and that when I make the change, you'll trust my judgment."

By this time, they're definitely worried. Maybe they've figured it out. Shoot up a quick prayer, my friend, and keep going.

"I'm not going to allow phones in bedrooms anymore at night."

Okay. You've said it. Remember to use the listening skills and tips for handling objections outlined in part 1. They'll doubtlessly feel this is unfair. It helps if you keep your reasons for the change focused on this being for their protection.

Personally, I (Tim) wouldn't leave phones in the kitchen overnight, as some families do. It's too tempting for teens to get up in the middle of the night to use theirs. My suggestion? Keep all the family phones in the parents' room at night.

"But I need my phone for the alarm in the morning." Be prepared for this by picking up a good old-fashioned alarm clock for them. Otherwise, *you'll* become their alarm clock every morning—and you don't want that.

Alternate Way to Say This

This issue is a big problem, and it may be worthwhile to go to extreme measures to institute this "no phones in bedrooms" policy with the least amount of resentment possible. Consider a variation of the Handoff approach in appendix A. Ask God to help you formulate an outside-the-box idea, like having someone (not you) ring your doorbell in the middle of the night to deliver mail to your teen. It would help make the point how a phone in their room—with messages coming all night—can hamper desperately needed sleep. And by asking someone else to ring the doorbell, you're not seen by your teen as the direct source of irritation. That's important if you hope to have a good conversation with them later.

When to Say This

If possible, catch them on a good day, when they're in a good mood. You'll need every advantage to help them accept this—especially if this is a change of family policy.

Ideally, avoid having this conversation right after they've messed up with their phone. They'll feel like you're punishing them. Like you're grounding them from their phone. Punishments end—or they should—unless you're being unfair. So, if they interpret taking their phone at night as a punishment, they'll see you as unfair if you don't give it back after a few days. No parent needs that.

When to Follow Up

As long as you keep your teen's phone in your room at night, you may think there's no need to follow up. But the purpose of your follow-up here is to make sure your teen isn't burning with resentment toward you.

Take them out to eat again. If they've handled this issue well at any point since your initial conversation, compliment them on it. Other than that, you don't have to talk about phones at all. Just make sure you're talking!

Someday they'll thank you for this . . . but don't hold your breath.

YOU REALIZE THE NEED TO LIMIT SCREEN TIME

Teenagers are on their phones. *A lot.* Their eyes stay glued to their screen while they walk, wait in line, are out with friends, are in the bathroom, are in bed, and as they sit at dinner. We've all seen students texting while riding their bikes or electric scooters! They're posting, updating, searching, texting, and, as a result, they're distracted at all times and in all places.

Why This Is Important

Let's look at a short list of why this matters.

- *Our phone is constantly setting the agenda for what we think about and focus on.* Colossians 3:2 says to "Set your minds on things that are above, not on things that are on earth" (ESV). That becomes increasingly difficult to do when we're consumed with streaming, scrolling, and getting notifications.
- *Much of what we see on our screens works directly against Philippians 4:8.* "Whatever is true, whatever is honorable, whatever is just, whatever is pure, whatever is lovely, whatever is commendable, if there is any excellence, if there is anything worthy of praise, think about these things" (ESV). If there's a story of someone pushed toward pure and excellent things after being on their phone, we'd love to hear about it!
- *Screen time influences who our teenagers are becoming and affects their habits.*
- *Screen time cultivates laziness and other bad effects of our teens' addiction that will follow them into their careers, marriages, parenthood, and every other facet of adulthood.*
- *Screen time fosters poor social habits, hurting our closest relationships.* When screens fill our days, eventually we tend to shortchange foundational relationships—like time with friends and family.
- *Screen time can push us toward isolation.* This isolation not only impacts teenagers mentally and emotionally but also gives their parents' voice and example less influence in their worldview and decision-making.
- *Screen time habits can impact our relationship with God.* Chances are, our teens already struggle to stay focused

during prayer and Bible reading. Add the distraction and pull of their phone to the mix, and what results is disjointed, unproductive time that makes it easy for teens to stop making time with God a priority.

There's more, but this is enough to show how much parents need to initiate this conversation. With our teens' peers, culture, and addictions, reducing screen time may sound like an impossible challenge. But it's worth the effort. We don't have to get the conversation perfect, but it matters that we have it.

WHAT TO SAY

First, check your own habits. This addiction isn't just a teen issue. Many parents struggle nearly as much. Nothing sabotages this conversation with your teenager like the hypocrisy of a double standard. Establish some hard lines and new goals for your own phone usage. The details of your plan come into play during your conversation with your teenager.

"I want to tell you about something I've been learning." Start with an admission of your phone overuse and the ways you've seen it impacting your attitude, thoughts, priorities, and habits. Share specific stories with them. Here's where you'll share why you think screen time matters and some of the concerns you see with these habits and addictions being formed. It'll be easier for them to receive this when you're talking about your own behavior instead of theirs.

"While I know it won't be easy, and I'm sure I'll mess up, I'm looking to make some changes for myself." Share specific ways you plan to cut back, what you hope that will do for you, and how it will benefit the family. It's good to emphasize that it will be as difficult for you, and there'll be moments when you won't get it right.

"How have you noticed screen time being an issue for you?" Most likely they'll have things to say. It's on you to listen carefully to their specific areas of struggle and how it's impacting them. If they aren't sure or don't think it *has* affected them, then you'll need to share your observations.

"**Here's what I am seeing.**" This is your opportunity to share specific examples of when you've seen them on their phones too much and how you see it affecting or hurting them. Two or three examples should be your max. They're probably already sensitive about this, and the last thing you want to do is pile on. If you've seen a progression happen over time, share that.

"**Let's brainstorm ideas for how you can effectively reduce screen time.**" Once again, being specific is everything. It won't be enough to say, "Try to watch fewer shows," or "You're on social media way too much." Your combined ideas should all be specific and measurable enough that they know what to aim for. Here are some ideas:

- *Set a time restriction for apps, with their input.* The restriction is set with a password that only you know as their parent. So, when they're out of time, they're locked out of that app.
- *Set restrictions for times when they can't be on their phone.* For example: at the dinner table, on the drive to/from school, not until after they do their full morning routine, not after 10:00 p.m.

"I want you to make these changes—just like I'm making changes—for the next month. I know these new limits will be hard for us at points, so we'll need to encourage each other to get to a better spot with this."

Alternate Way to Say This

Check out the Game/Challenge approach or the Let's Brainstorm Creative Alternates approach in appendix A. These alternates help put us on their side/team as we work out a solution.

When to Say This

Maybe we should start with when *not* to say this. Like at the end of the day. You want this conversation to have the time it needs for a full discussion. Also, teens tend to be on their phones the most at night. It will feel more like an attack and less like a helpful correction.

This conversation is big and serious enough to dedicate legitimate time to it. Invite them out for coffee or a walk. Let them know you want to talk through a few things you're looking to change. That gives them a heads-up to be ready to talk and signals that the topic is important enough to set aside time for it.

When to Follow Up

Remember, they aren't the only ones working to cut some screen time. You're doing this together! It's natural to ask them about it after a week or two. Share with them when it has been most difficult for you. Use this as a chance to encourage them and keep them focused on the goal.

If you see them fail, you can't overlook it. You want to follow up in that moment with encouragement. At the end of the month, schedule another talk with specific questions:

- What was most challenging about our new habits?
- What were positive differences you noticed in yourself in the last month? How about in me?
- What do you think we need to add or take away from what we did this last month to make sure we keep doing this moving forward?

WARNING TEENS BEFORE THEY GET INVOLVED IN PORN

Three big reasons parents don't talk to their kids about the dangers of pornography:

- The topic is incredibly uncomfortable.
- Parents don't believe porn is an issue for *their* teens.
- Parents don't want their *own* struggle with porn, past or present, revealed.

The effects of porn can be so devastating, we don't dare avoid this talk for any reason. If we have a history with pornography, we know the dangers. The enemy wants us to leave our kids unprotected. We can't listen to him.

Let's aim for three things in this conversation:

- To help our sons and daughters understand why porn is so bad.
- To help them know how to avoid porn.
- To help them know what to do if they've been exposed to porn.

On a side note: You're talking to your teen about the importance of waiting for sex until marriage, right? This can be a huge topic involving lust, masturbation, sexting, getting physically involved with someone, and so on. Too many Christians compromise the clear biblical standards—and reap the consequences. We don't want that for our kids, so let's be sure we're talking about saving sex for marriage. This issue about porn absolutely needs to be part of that conversation.

Why This Is Important

There are so many good things we want for our teens.

- To grow into men and women of character and integrity.
- To be true to the Lord and not lead a fake, double life.
- To be happily married someday.

Porn attacks every one of those areas with deadly accuracy. It has the power to undo all the good things we want for our kids. Every single one.

We may do everything possible to insulate our kids from porn, and that's good. But if they have a phone, or have friends who own one? Porn will find our teens, even if they aren't looking. Our enemy is extremely good at that. We want to prepare our kids for that moment and help them run from porn.

This isn't just something to talk to our sons about. Countless girls are being drawn into porn and need to understand the truth about it too. Even if we're certain our daughters would never view porn, we need to talk to them anyway. Their friends are very likely into porn—or they'll date somebody who has been into porn. Our daughters need to understand that porn is a sin and extremely dangerous.

WHAT TO SAY

Focus on porn being an enemy weapon meant to destroy us. Placing the emphasis *there* at the start takes the spotlight off your teen, to an extent, and puts it on the forces of darkness that strategize to take them down.

"You know Mom/Dad want you to be a person who loves and obeys God. You also know our enemy, the devil and his demons, strategize to destroy you—and rob you of experiencing all God's best for you, right?

Our enemy has developed a weapon that has taken out countless others, and I want to warn you about it. That weapon is pornography in all its forms."

There. You said it. Good job. Now, make sure they understand what pornography is.

"Pornography—or porn—is any sort of sexual pictures, videos, actions, or writing that is meant to excite or arouse a person.

Here are four reasons why porn is so toxic.

1. God says sex is for marriage—solely between a husband and wife. Porn encourages sex outside of marriage. Disobeying God always leads to tragedy.
2. Porn is built on lust, not love. Lust is twisted, selfish sex. If we expose ourselves to that, we become twisted and selfish. What do you think that might do to your marriage someday?
3. Choosing to do things we know are wrong, like viewing porn, quenches the work of the Holy Spirit in our lives, which keeps us from growing as Christians. How dangerous would it be if that happened to us?
4. Like drugs, porn is highly addictive. Porn can actually alter your brain. You'll crave more. That means disobeying God more, twisting your view of sex more, and causing more tragedy."

"How do you think kids get exposed to porn?" Get input from your teen. Here are some prompts if you need them.

- Phones.
- Friends. Some friends may actually *try* to expose you to porn. They may send you texts of naked pictures or ask you to send naked pictures of yourself.
- Some music and video games.

Talking about these should also lead to talking about the obvious . . . how they can avoid exposing themselves to porn in each of the above examples.

"What do you do if you've been exposed to porn? Talk to Mom/Dad. It's easy to think porn doesn't hurt anyone, but it does. Let us help you take the next right steps so that porn doesn't mess you up."

Mom, Dad . . . if you want to help your kids, you need to know if they've been exposed to porn. The key to getting your teen to open up? Make it EASY for them to talk to you.

"When was the last time you saw something that might be considered porn?"

Instead of asking them *if* they've ever seen porn—a question that may prompt a knee-jerk reaction to cover up—calmly pose the question as if you expect they *have* been exposed. It's crucial they can tell by your tone or by the look in your eyes that you're not angry with them.

They need to sense that you love them so much, you only want to help them.

You'll know by their answer, nonanswer, and body language if they've seen porn. You'll know how to take it from there, and you'll probably want to reference the suggestions in the very next scenario in this book, "You Suspect or Know Your Teen Is into Porn."

Alternate Way to Say This

This conversation about porn needs to happen. If for some reason you can't do it, you need to find someone who can talk to your teen about this . . . soon. Check the Handoff approach as described in appendix A. Another option would be the Object Lesson approach. A great choice from the book *The Very Best, Hands-On,*

Kinda Dangerous Family Devotions, vol. 3 would be "Porn: Toxic. Twisting. Trap."

When to Say This

Today. Tomorrow. *This* week . . . not next. If you're not sure your teen is old enough or ready for this topic, it's more likely *you're* not ready. The best option may be to start our defensive strategy early by talking to our kids about this when they're nine or ten years old. Before they get exposed. Our kids are easy targets for the enemy . . . and we'd rather err on the side of warning them too early than too late.

Because this topic is so uncomfortable, review chapter 1, "Prepping for the Talk with Your Teen," especially the tips under the heading "The Atmosphere Is Important."

When to Follow Up

This is definitely not a one-and-done talk. You'll need to follow up early and often. Our enemy is relentless. We dare not think that one talk with our teens is enough to protect them—especially if they've been exposed.

After the initial talk, try to follow up within a week. The longer you wait, the easier it gets *not* to talk about it. Then maybe bring it up about once a month after that. The topic will become easier and easier to talk about, and your teen will become more comfortable with being honest with you.

As you have this talk—with God's help—know that we're cheering you on. There may not be one in ten Christian parents who will tackle this topic adequately. But you're doing it. You're protecting your kids, which is exactly what God designed you to do. Good job, my friend!

YOU SUSPECT OR KNOW YOUR TEEN IS INTO PORN

Recently, I (Mark) surveyed high school students from a solid church youth group. Students knew their responses were absolutely anonymous. Here's one of the questions I asked:

Have you seen nudity on Snapchat?

One hundred percent of the male and female students answered *YES*. Whether accidentally or not, all of them had seen porn—which often develops an appetite for more.

Our teens need our help.

Why This Is Important

The Bible is clear: Pornography is wrong. Now, our teens may say that images of people naked or having sex weren't even around in Bible times, so how can the Bible speak against pornography? The Bible has much to say about steering clear of prostitutes (those having sex for some kind of personal gain or money—or because someone else is profiting from them) and adulterers (those having sex with someone other than their spouse for any reason). People who create pornography today are in the business of prostitution. They're selling sex outside of marriage. The Bible has so much to say about the dangers to anyone—like our teens—who get sucked into their trap. We're to run from sexual sin, and that includes viewing images of those engaged in it.

Porn can destroy our teens and destroy their marriages someday. The previous scenario, "Warning Teens Before They Get Involved in Porn," included a short list of some of the dangers porn brings to our teens. Take a look at that again; it will help you do the tough job of talking to your teen about this. They desperately need your help—even though they rarely realize it.

WHAT TO SAY

You want to make it easy for your teen to be honest with you. The key is in your tone and approach. If it seems like you're confronting them, their natural tendency will be to lie. That won't help anyone. Start the conversation by calmly making the assumption that they've seen porn.

"Pornography is more accessible now than ever before. When was the last time you saw a naked image of someone?"

Give them a moment. If they don't answer, you probably *have* your answer.

"Where did you see that image?"

It's important to know the source; you'll use that information later to help them set up safeguards in that area.

"Pornography rewires the brain, in a sense. It creates a craving for sex in ways God didn't intend. And the brain becomes more focused on finding ways to experience more and more porn. It's absolutely like drug addiction. The Bible warns of the dangers of getting sucked in by prostitutes and those involved in sex outside marriage—and that includes watching them on a screen. Let's look at Proverbs 7:24–27:

> Now then, my sons, listen to me;
> pay attention to what I say.
> Do not let your heart turn to her [adulterous] ways
> or stray into her paths.
> Many are the victims she has brought down;
> her slain are a mighty throng.
> *Her house is a highway to the grave,*
> *leading down to the chambers of death.* (emphasis added)

So many people act like porn is harmless. But these verses talk about it being a 'highway to the grave.' What kinds of death might result from staying on a path of viewing porn?"

Here are some prompts if you need them.

- **"Death of respect."** People into porn—especially as they grow into adults—often lose the respect of those closest to them. Their spouse. Kids. Friends. And, eventually, themselves.
- **"Death of relationships."** Someday your teen will likely be married—and their mate will know if they're viewing porn. They'll see it as a huge break of trust . . . as unfaithfulness. You doubtlessly know stories of marriages that died because of porn. Share them with your teen.
- **"Death of dreams."** People into porn have a craving to get their next hit of porn. Their focus shifts. Whatever dreams they had become eclipsed by their increasing desire for porn.
- **"Death of God's plan for your life."** Those who won't let go of their sin are distancing themselves from God, and consequently his plan for them.

"Son/daughter, porn will destroy all those who stay on its path."

Remember, when quoting Scripture, you need to speak it in love—not use it as a club.

> Flee from sexual immorality. All other sins a person commits are outside the body, but whoever sins sexually, sins against their own body. (1 Cor. 6:18)

"Can we talk about breaking free?" If your teen sincerely wants to be free of pornography's death grip, be prepared with some specific steps for them to take. There are many "how-to" lists that outline a path to freedom but don't actually work. They emphasize the wrong things or have the order upside down. Sure, you can put filters on their phone, and so on, but without heart change, your teen will find ways around such things. Here's a short list of things your teen will need to do—and this list *works*. These things may sound cliché, but they're effective. Why? Because they are about spending time with God, and they're totally rooted in heart change.

1. *Confess to God that they've sinned in this area and ask for his forgiveness.* They'll need to repent and make the decision to no longer view porn.
2. *Pray and surrender to the Holy Spirit's control.* Your teen needs heart change. A change of desires. That's one of the specialties of the Holy Spirit. This involves surrender . . . your teen *asking* the Holy Spirit to change their desires. The Holy Spirit also gives supernatural self-control to run from temptation as he changes our hearts, right?
3. *Renew their mind.* This is all about being in the Word regularly so they don't forget or stray from the truth (Rom. 12:1–2). And not just reading the Bible but putting it into practice as Jesus explained in Matthew 7:24–28. As your teen reads about the dangers of sexual sin (it's all over Proverbs) and about the joy and strength of abiding with God, that's good soil for heart change. Look at John 15 together. While sexual sin brings death, this chapter talks about God bringing fruit in our lives (something very alive) as we abide in Christ through prayer and time in his Word. As we do this, God brings life to us and changes our hearts and desires away from death and toward new life.
4. *Strengthen their self-control.* This means saying no to opportunities to see porn and removing the sources for easy access to porn. They need to set up boundaries.

Remember when you asked where they had last viewed a naked image? This is where you want to help them set up restrictions in that area. Self-control is needed . . . and yet, self-control alone is not enough.

5. *Accountability.* You'll want to make a pact with your teen that you'll ask them regularly how they're doing with the porn issue—and they must promise to be 100 percent honest.

Alternate Way to Say This

Maybe you feel your teen needs to talk to someone other than you. Check out the Ask the Expert approach as described in appendix A. The Field Trip approach could also be a great option. Imagine taking your teen to a local funeral home, city morgue, or cemetery for a tour—and reading Proverbs 7:24–27 to them there, along with Romans 6:11–16.

As Christians, we're dead to sin, but when we hang out in places of the dead (Prov. 7:24–27) it's like we're digging up these buried sins and infusing them with life. We can become slaves to sin again, and that kind of slavery is absolutely terrifying!

When to Say This

Once you sense you need to talk to your teen about this, consider that a prompt from the Lord. You'll want to obey quickly. Within a few days. You only want to take as much time as it requires to decide on how you'll approach this scenario—and to prep for that talk.

Remember, teens are more likely to talk when they don't feel like their faces can be seen as easily. So maybe you have this talk at bedtime, with you sitting on the edge of their bed. Or maybe this talk will happen best during a drive where they can stare out the side window and know they aren't being studied.

When to Follow Up

Our teens are often addicted to porn long before they realize it. We'll need to check back with them regularly on this, and we'll need to help them break free—and stay free.

Mom, Dad, are you enslaved with porn yourself? Break free with God's help. Your kids desperately need you to, so you can help them. Grab hold of the five steps above with both hands.

I (Tim) have heard speakers at men's conferences tell audiences that they'd always struggle with lust or porn.

That's not true.

The Bible says God sets prisoners free.

This is what we want for our teens, and it starts with having this talk.

9

FRIENDS OR DATING

ASKING TO STAY OVERNIGHT AT A FRIEND'S— BUT YOU DON'T APPROVE

If our teens want to stay overnight at a friend or relative's home, and deep down we don't feel comfortable about it? Let's trust our gut. We should not allow our kids or other adults to guilt us into thinking that a good parent would let this overnighter happen.

Why This Is Important

Here's a few reminders to help us stick to our convictions instead of crumbling and giving in against our better judgment.

- *How well do we know this friend?* If we don't know them well, we already have all the information we need to say no to the overnighter.
- *Who else will be at the overnighter?* Even if we know our son or daughter's friend well, do we know everyone else

who will be staying overnight? One person can steer the events of the night in a really bad direction.
- *What kind of parental supervision will be present?* Will a mom and dad be there? Do they share our same standards—and the dedication to make sure those standards are followed? Will at least one parent stay up as long as the kids are awake, just to check on them?
- *Do we know the parents?* Regularly we hear news of some adult—even church leaders—whose carefully hidden dark side came out and caused tremendous damage and heartache. As parents, it's our job to protect our kids. If we have a nagging concern, let's not dismiss it.
- *What's the plan for the evening?* Honestly, even if we were given a typed schedule of events for the night, plans have a way of changing when teenagers are involved. Will someone call to get our approval if things change?
- *Overnighters often expose decent kids to indecent things.* Movies. Activities. Conversations. Inappropriate games. Daring each other to do things we would never allow. Texting with other teens in ways that turn sexual—like pressure to send nude photos. Bullying takes place during overnighters in subtle ways. Our teens are often encouraged to do things that normally they wouldn't even dream of.
- *Is the home safe in other ways?* If there are firearms, for example, are they kept in a locked gun safe?

WHAT TO SAY

Chances are, if your teen is invited for an overnighter, they'll ask for your permission at a bad time for you to make the best decision. Teens are smart that way. They may ask at the last minute or when you're distracted—whenever you're more likely to give your permission without fully thinking it through.

Sometimes you need to stall the conversation until you've had a chance to think, pray, talk to your spouse, and maybe even take a fresh look at this section of the book.

"Let's talk about this tonight when I can give you my full attention and I've had some time to think this through a bit."

If they pressure you for a decision right there on the spot, they might as well be waving a big yellow or red flag. You definitely need to proceed with caution.

If you say, "Let's talk tonight," that's what you need to do.

Imagine you have to say no when that talk actually starts. Realize your tone will make or break this. You might start out this way: **"I hate having to say no on this, because I know you'd really like to do it. But there's a part of me—that parent part—that is warning me that this isn't a good idea. I can say yes and maybe get a nice hug from you, but I wouldn't be doing the job God gave me to do."**

This news can be crushing to a teen. You want to show some empathy—even though that doesn't change your decision.

They may ask for your reasoning, but odds are they won't be in much of a mindset to receive your convictions on this. That doesn't mean you don't explain. You should. But you have to be realistic. Even if you lay out your concerns, likely based on things listed in the "Why This Is Important" section above, you may not get that hug afterward.

Alternate Way to Say This

This would be a great example of a conversation you'd want to move into the Let's Brainstorm approach in appendix A. When my (Tim's) kids were growing up, we learned some good lessons about the dangers of overnighters at a friend's house. But we brainstormed an alternate solution: allowing a sleepover—as long as it was at *our* home. That way, we got to know their friends better, and we felt we were doing our best to protect our kids.

And we did everything we could to make sleepovers at our home *fun*. That meant having plenty of snacks and favorite treats and doing everything possible to create an atmosphere where our kids *wanted* their sleepovers to be at our home—and their friends did too.

When to Say This

If our kids received an invitation for an overnighter, we'll probably need to give them an answer the same day they ask for our permission. Stalling will only exasperate them. If we're not a fan of our kids sleeping over at the home of a friend, the best way to avoid stress and drama is to talk about this long before there's an invitation for a sleepover. We simply explain to our kids the family rules about sleepovers: We won't allow them to stay at a friend's, but when they're old enough, they can have friends at our house.

Note: Unless you're raising your kids as a single parent, be sure to talk this out with your spouse. You need to be united on the issue—or your teen will work one parent against the other. Similarly, you have to be careful not to make your spouse look like the bad person when your kid asks to stay overnight at a friend's home. In other words, never say this: "It's okay with me, but you'll have to ask your mom/dad about that."

When to Follow Up

If you say no to an overnighter—and it hasn't been switched to your house? That means the overnighter may still be happening with other kids while your teen is at home. Realize your teen is thinking about it plenty. They're likely getting texts or seeing the fun they're missing on social media. It would be hard to imagine any teen being okay with that.

Be very intentional about making that night fun for your teen. Ideally, plan something for that night that makes it special. Is there another friend of theirs who wasn't invited to the sleepover that your teen can invite to your home? Set something in motion. Is there a new movie your teen would really like to see? Pay the streaming rental fee or take them to the theater.

And if you offered to have a sleepover at your house but it didn't work this time? Be sure to encourage your teen to invite someone over in the next couple of weeks. That will give them something to look forward to.

YOU'RE NOT COMFORTABLE WITH THE FRIENDS YOUR TEEN CHOOSES

As parents, there's one kind of personal weight loss we hate: when we lose some weight of *influence* with our teens. Our opinions, concerns, instructions, and approval don't hold nearly as much weight as they once did. The friends our teens choose are their major influencers now, for good or for bad.

Why This Is Important

The perspective, morals, habits, behavior, or beliefs of the friends our teens choose will influence them massively. The possibility of friends steering our teens in potentially bad or harmful directions is enough to put this scenario high on our priority list of topics to cover.

WHAT TO SAY

Remember, your ability to influence your teen may be weaker than it's ever been. A parent must be wise. Patient. Simply forbidding a friendship rarely works. Think of a fisher reeling in a five-hundred-pound tuna on a fifty-pound test line. If you aren't smart about this, you'll snap the line—and lose whatever pull you have with your teen.

So, before confronting your teen about their friends, gather a little intel first.

- Have your teen invite their friend to your house—and purposely hang around to get to know them. Make it fun. Have food; maybe you make your teen's favorite treat. That helps make the friend feel welcome. Feeding their friends well creates a great first impression.
- Bring your teen and their friend to a play, game, movie, or restaurant.

As you get to know that friend, you may find *you* can influence that friend for good. Wouldn't that be terrific? At the very least, you'll see if your concerns are real—and if you need to take it to the next step.

"Your friend (name): Tell me what you like about them." Tone is important here. If you sound like you're looking for ammo, the conversation won't go well. If you've gotten to know their friend, now you can share qualities you like too. This is really, really important to do before you express concerns.

"There are also things about (name) that scare/concern me a bit. Promise me you'll be careful, okay?" Again, watch your tone. If you speak in love, you'll reduce the chances of them feeling they need to defend their friend. If you sound unreasonably biased, you're going to snap that fishing line. They'll likely ask what concerns you. You have two options here:

1. Carefully share.
2. Don't share your concerns. *Yet*. Unless your relationship with your teen is super strong, it may be best to

try this approach: **"I'm not sure I want to get into specifics just yet. Sometimes I get a feeling. Just keep your eyes open, okay? I can share things, but I'd rather wait until you've had a chance to observe a bit more yourself."**

There's power in this course of action. You're trusting your teen to look more closely at their friendships. And you won't look like you're in a hurry to say something negative about their friend.

Alternate Way to Say This

This would be a great example of a conversation you'd want to move into the Handoff approach in appendix A. Sometimes your relationship with your teen isn't strong enough for this conversation. Rather than risk weakening it further, consider who might be respected enough to speak into their life a bit. A grandparent? An aunt or uncle? A youth pastor? Or maybe you know someone who was burned in a bad friendship, and you know they can tackle the topic with your teen in a way that'll get through.

When to Say This

Often an incident will trigger this conversation. Maybe your teen made a bad decision after being influenced by a friend, and you have to address it right away. You'll have to work extra hard to be sure you're saying everything in love.

Or maybe you're having a good day with your teen—and that may provide a good opportunity.

There may be no "good" time to talk to your teen about this. But if you have concerns, you dare not stall for long. Just be sure you're prayed-up and ready before starting.

When to Follow Up

If you've brought up some concerns about your teen's friend, give it a week before bringing it up again. Otherwise, they'll think you're hounding them on the topic. And you've probably created little shadows of doubt about their friend. This gives your teen time to observe and process things a bit too.

In the meantime . . .

- Keep praying your teen's eyes will be opened to the dangers of this friendship.
- Continue to look for ways to bring that friend into your world so you and your family can influence them—and protect your teen.
- Create opportunities for your teen to meet others who would be the kind of friend they need. Can you be more dedicated to getting your teen involved with the youth group at church? Sure, they can still make some bad friendships there, but the likelihood of finding a good friend may be a bit higher. Wherever you bring them to meet other kids, you still need to be aware and involved when it comes to the friends your teen chooses.
- Consider asking a youth pastor for help. Maybe they can introduce your teen to someone in the youth group who'd be a good influence.
- Can you talk to that youth group teen yourself and ask if they'd reach out to your son or daughter? This sounds risky, but it can be done successfully. The greater risks are the consequences of what may happen if your teen fails to make better friends.

When you're careful and wise with how you handle this issue of friends, your weight as an influencer goes up. That's encouraging, isn't it? May all of us gain plenty of that kind of weight as parents!

What if nothing changes? What if, after all that, your teen still clings tight to the friendship that has you concerned, you haven't been able to influence their friend, and you're more convinced than ever that the friendship is destructive? What can you do to reel your teen in a bit—without snapping that line?

- *Lay it all out before God in prayer.* This is what King Hezekiah did in 2 Kings 19. He was up against a situation too big for him—and God delivered. Read the story. God can come up with all kinds of creative solutions we've never dreamed of.
- *Lay your concerns out before your teen in a humble (not authoritative) way.* This is what King Solomon did more than once in Proverbs. "Listen, my son, to your father's instruction and do not forsake your mother's teaching" (Prov. 1:8). Can you sense the earnest, heartfelt plea in this? It's all about the tone.
- *Look at the calendar.* Are they just months from graduation, and this bad influence will be moving away soon? If so, you might choose to hang tight and pray hard.
- *Do the thing you believe deep down you should do, but don't want to.* If this influence on your teen is really bad—dangerously so—what would you be willing to do to distance your teen from them? Chances are, there's something in your mind right now. Take the car keys away? Move your teen to a new school? Move the family to a new state? Take a leave of absence from your job and travel with your teen for a month? Yes, these are drastic, but if the stakes are high, we're talking a last-ditch effort here. Pray. Test it. Get advice from trusted and wise people in your life. See if your drastic measure is from the Lord. If so, move forward to rescue your teen—even if you fear the line might snap.

YOUR TEEN THINKS THEY'RE READY TO DATE—BUT YOU DON'T

I (Mark) started working as a youth pastor when I was twenty-four. The problem was, I looked more like a seventeen-year-old student. Parents and students would say, "*You* are the leader?"

Even worse was the fact that one of my students, Ian, looked like he was in his upper twenties. He had more facial hair than me, more muscle mass, a deeper voice . . . you get the point. At times, people assumed Ian was the youth pastor and I was the student.

He loved it. But even though he looked the part, he wasn't qualified to *be* the youth pastor. Nothing against Ian, but he just wasn't ready for a lot of reasons, like age, experience, and training.

As our teenagers physically mature, they'll believe they're ready to date. But just because they hit a certain age or look old enough, that doesn't mean they're ready.

Why This Is Important

If our teens date before they're ready to do it right, life-changing pain and regret often follow. We don't want that for our teens.

Most of our teens will want to date for one or more of the following reasons:

- physical attraction
- they like someone
- status
- it feels grown-up
- friends are dating
- for fun/distraction/experience
- for emotional support
- physical pleasure/thrills

None of these should be the main reason to start dating. What our teenagers need is a good understanding of the purpose of dating. When they build on that foundation, it sets a good course for the rest of the relationship.

WHAT TO SAY

You'll want to let them know in advance that you're planning to talk about dating. Otherwise, they may feel blindsided or embarrassed.

"**What are some reasons you see people start dating?**"

If you're in a restaurant, grab a napkin and make a list together. Likely the list resembles the one in the previous section.

"**What do you think God would say is the purpose for dating?**"

Dating is about finding the Christian person who would make a good spouse from God's point of view. They'd need to be a strong believer, right? Fully dedicated to the Lord. They'd need to have the character qualities that would make them a great mate. Brainstorm some qualities like these with your teen.

"**When we date, we're testing a friendship to see if that person would one day be a good choice for us to marry.**" Whoa. They may think that sounds a bit too serious. But that's the point: Dating *is* serious.

"**Why is it you'd like to turn this friendship into a dating relationship?**" This isn't asked in an accusatory way. You genuinely want to understand their purpose in dating and see if it matches God's.

"**If God's purpose for dating (finding a Christian who would be a good choice to marry) isn't your main goal right now, then it's not a good idea to enter into this relationship. Does that make sense?**"

Our purposes for dating should always be done with God's ultimate destination in mind. If the person your teen wants to date is someone they can't see marrying, then they shouldn't pursue it. If they do, their purpose is wrong—and it will lead your teen to places they were never supposed to go.

As a parent, your reasons for not allowing dating yet must be specific and motivated by love. At this point in the conversation, you'll probably get the most pushback. Take your time explaining your thinking and do plenty of listening. They might know you're right, but it takes them time to accept that.

There's a chance they'll *say* the right things. They truly believe they're ready to test a friendship over the course of time to see if that person would be a good fit for marriage. Good. Compliment them. But if you still feel they're not ready to date with God's goal of dating in mind, this is your chance to explain.

"Let's make another list, but this time let's list things that may indicate a person isn't ready to date."

Get their input. Below are some prompts.

- *Age/maturity*: I wouldn't set an age when they can automatically date. But I'd say that it is rare for younger teenagers to have the right focus within dating. They're too many years away from a marrying age.
- *Dishonesty*: They've kept the relationship a secret from their parents and have been texting each other or sneaking to see each other.
- *Imbalance*: They've isolated themselves from other friends and family in the friendship phase.
- *Boundaries*: They don't have adequate personal convictions or a list of boundaries they will not cross physically with a date.
- *Self-control*: They lack self-control, and the relationship has already gotten physical.
- *Faith*: Their relationship with God isn't in a good spot, and their ability to make good decisions and keep their focus on him in the relationship isn't there.

- *Rebellion*: They aren't being respectful or responsible, or they aren't honoring Mom or Dad the way they should. Our teens need to be open with us and demonstrate a willingness to talk about their lives so that we can help them—especially in this area of dating.
- *Porn*: If a teen is involved in porn in any way, they do not possess the self-control or the right priorities to date anyone.

If anything on this list above describes your teen, letting them date would put them on a collision course with potential sin and all its consequences. It's like letting a toddler drive your car. That toddler will drive aimlessly—unable to control the power of the vehicle—until it slams into a wall.

IMPORTANT NOTE: You can't just leave it at "You're not ready to date." You'll exasperate your teen, making them more prone to rebel. Develop a plan to help them work on these areas and get ready for dating.

In the meantime, you can encourage them to build a stronger friendship with the person they're interested in.

"Dating can be so good, and you'll get to that point. In the meantime, there's so much good that can come from building into friendships with people of the opposite sex. I want you to focus on that and experience the goodness there."

You want them to learn how to form healthy bonds with the opposite sex, and you can emphasize the benefits of that.

"What's your plan for how you'll stay just friends?" Your teenager might have already started moving toward dating, so how do they pull back? Help them figure this out. You really don't want them getting advice from friends or the internet.

It's important to encourage your teen to invite their friend over to the house—often. Family night. Movie night. Family outings. This encourages the friendship and lets you speak into the life of their friend as well.

Alternate Way to Say This

Check out the Field Trip approach in appendix A. There's also an outing in *The Very Best, Hands-On, Kinda Dangerous Family Devotions*, vol. 3 called "Beauty Is a Beast." It's powerful!

When to Say This

Do this one at a decent restaurant over dinner. Eating together gives you and your teen something to do while having the conversation—and the natural interruptions might ease tensions. A restaurant keeps the conversation from getting rushed too.

When to Follow Up

If there are things they're working on to show they're ready to date, follow up soon. If they're putting someone in the friend zone (after pulling back from thinking of them being in the boy/girlfriend zone), follow up right after that happens so you can process with them. Regardless, check in a few days later and casually ask if they've had any more thoughts about your conversation.

YOUR TEEN WANTS TO DATE A NON-CHRISTIAN

Conversations where teens feel their parents dictate who they can and can't marry don't seem to go well. Cue the clip of Ariel and King Triton from the 1989 animated movie *The Little Mermaid*.

- Daughter wants to marry a human. *"Daddy, I love him."*
- Dad tries talking sense into her. *"He's a human, you're a mermaid!"*[*]

---

[*]*The Little Mermaid*, directed by Ron Clements and John Musker (Walt Disney Pictures, 1989), 00:35:40.

An all-out argument ensues, which leads to Ariel rebelling—and scheming to see that young man behind Dad's back.

I know, I know, it's a fairy tale. But in the very real story of your teen's life, this dating issue is a critical yet potentially volatile conversation, and sometimes it goes bad.

Why This Is Important

The Bible doesn't have specific passages about dating. They were more into the arranged marriage thing. But God *did* warn parents against allowing kids to marry anyone except a follower of the one true God.

> You shall not intermarry with them, giving your daughters to their sons or taking their daughters for your sons, for they would turn away your sons from following me, to serve other gods. (Deut. 7:3–4 ESV)

Is that just an Old Testament thing? Not at all.

> Do not be unequally yoked with unbelievers. For what partnership has righteousness with lawlessness? Or what fellowship has light with darkness? What accord has Christ with Belial? Or what portion does a believer share with an unbeliever? (2 Cor. 6:14–15 ESV)

God puts one big boundary on marriage. Our choice must be a believer. So, if a teenager is dating a non-Christian, they're already heading in the one direction God has forbidden. That's not a great start.

The Bible has lots to say about the purpose of marriage, which makes sense. God created it, and he gets to set the rules for how it works. Since dating is our modern-day route to marriage, we should date people who fit the qualifications for marriage.

Why does God care who we marry? The oneness of marriage is powerful. The person who *doesn't* follow God will generally influence the one who does, turning their heart away. They won't follow God as fully as they would if both were Christians. If you're wondering if that will *really* happen, check out the story of King Solomon in 1 Kings 11. Even the wisest man who ever lived couldn't stop it from happening.

This heart change begins in the dating relationship. When a Christian dates a non-Christian, too often their godly values are compromised and their life purpose and priorities change.

WHAT TO SAY

Ideally, you'll have this conversation with your teen long before they're of dating age—or interested in someone who isn't truly following God. But if you've missed that boat, here's the next best place to launch.

"I know you're excited about this relationship. Tell me some things you like about him/her." Listen so you hear what really matters to them. You want to understand your teen. As that happens, you'll become a better teacher, helping them get to where they need to be.

"You mentioned some great stuff there. How much have you two talked about your faith and what that means to you?" So often, faith, God, church, and Christianity have only been a brief, awkward conversation—if at all. Rarely have these young people conveyed to each other their beliefs and what role faith plays in their lives. If they're dating and getting to know each other, shouldn't they talk about something that is central to their lives?

"I'm concerned about this relationship because this person hasn't met the main nonnegotiable requirement of someone you can marry." This is where you can talk through some of the points covered in "Why This Is Important" above.

"I want to help you visualize what's happening here." There are so many ways to illustrate how dating a non-Christian will pull them in the opposite direction God wants for them. One time, when I (Mark) taught this to a group of high schoolers, I tied two couples together by their ankles. One couple was tied facing the same direction in traditional three-legged race fashion. The other couple faced opposite directions. I had both pairs navigate through a crowded room as quickly as they could. The conclusion was obvious. The couple facing the same direction was far better off. The other couple fell, got frustrated, and finished far behind. That's what it's like when we date someone who has a different set of priorities and way of thinking about the world.

"I love and support you, but I can't support this relationship. Do you have any reason I should change my mind?" Here are the top three answers teens usually give, along with some responses you might offer. Your tone and listening skills are critical here. (Take a pause to quickly review chapter 1, "Prepping for the Talk with Your Teen." It'll take only minutes, but could save you hours of grief, heartache, and regret.)

1. "But we aren't even thinking about getting married; we're just dating."

    "The purpose of dating is to get to know someone better to see if they're someone you would marry. Dating is not just about having fun. Dating is not just about gaining some kind of social status by dating a particular person. And dating is definitely not about satisfying our desires to experience something physically or emotionally with them. If this person, as they are now, is already disqualified by God as a marriage candidate for you as a Christian, why would you keep dating them?"

2. "But I'm going to share the gospel with them as we date. They'll probably become a Christian, but if they don't, we'll break up."

"I love your heart to share the gospel with them, but you can do that as their friend. You don't need to be their boy/girlfriend. I appreciate you wanting to influence them for good, but can you see how you're also opening yourself up to being influenced by them? Also, the longer you date, the harder it will be to break up. There'll be genuinely great things you love about them. To delay a breakup until later in the hope that they get saved is setting yourself up for a very hard decision. It's so difficult to do that many people compromise and stay together—and end up missing so much."

3. "I get that they aren't a Christian, but they're honestly a better person than most Christians I know."

    "It sounds like they're a great person with lots of great qualities. I'm glad you want to marry someone who has good character. But if they aren't a Christian, their purpose in life and perspective on so many things are—or will be—different from yours. How they think about marriage, kids, money, careers, church, friendships, and more will all be different. They might be a good person, but they have a different mission and purpose. And they don't have the Holy Spirit to grow them with love, joy, peace, kindness, and so on."

The key here is to take these questions on calmly and firmly, helping them see the truth, which will hopefully help them be ready for what you say next.

"Do you understand why you need to end this relationship?" This is a big moment. They might stand firm and continue to argue. If they do, you will go back to listening and lovingly correcting them. But hopefully, at this point, they'll see it and agree with you.

"Let's talk through how you should break up with them in the most honorable way." Many teenagers don't know how to end a relationship. They send texts, just ignore the person, or have the conversation but are just plain rude. You want to teach them how to do this well. Remember, they'll be nervous about the talk. Take the time to support them.

Do you have a teen dating someone who won't take no for an answer? Remember, your teen may need extra help with exactly what to say, how to say it, and what to do as they move forward with this.

Alternate Way to Say This

Check out the Object Lesson approach in appendix A. Did you buy *The Very Best, Hands-On, Kinda Dangerous Family Devotions* books? If so, consider "Three-Legged Race" in volume 2.

When to Say This

This conversation needs privacy from siblings. Choose a time and place where your teen will know they can speak freely. Otherwise, they won't be as open with you.

This isn't a rushed conversation on a ten-minute drive—or as they get ready for prom. You need to allow plenty of time to hear them so you can strategically help them.

You also can't wait a few weeks or months in the hope they figure it out themselves. The minute you know they like someone who isn't saved, make plans to have this conversation. It will be far easier if you have the conversation *before* they've officially started dating.

When to Follow Up

Your first follow-up should be within a week of your first talk. They've had plenty of time to think through what you've said. They might have more rebuttals, and that's fine. Don't be discouraged by that. At least you're having the conversation—and getting the opportunity to steer them in a better direction.

If they're still resisting, consider asking them to talk to someone else, perhaps a youth pastor or family member they respect. Do you know someone who married a non-Christian, and while they love their mate, they've experienced how hard it can be? If they have the right tone, they can relate to your teen in ways you can't. Hearing truth from a few different people has a way of getting through to a hard heart.

One last thought . . . and this is tough. If you see they aren't listening to you and aren't ending the relationship, this reveals exactly where their heart is: They're pushing back against your wishes and God's commands. The real issue is bigger than them wanting to date a non-Christian. Your focus moves from being solely about "getting them to break up" to including the lack of spiritual growth in their life. Check the scenarios in the next section of this book that talk about growing in the faith.

10

THEIR WALK WITH GOD

YOUR TEEN DOESN'T WANT TO GO TO CHURCH

The Sunday morning wrestling match. We wake our teens, and they assure us they're getting up. But when we return ten minutes later, they're still in bed.

We might wonder if the fight is worth it. With their attitude, they won't get anything out of church anyway. We'd have a lot less stress—and there'd be less tension between us and our teens—if we let them drop back into their bed and left without them.

Why This Is Important

At church, as we worship, everyone also has two jobs to do—*including* our teens.

- We're to encourage others.
- We're to help inspire others to stay on the right path.

That means others will be doing these things for us and for our teens. When our teens aren't at church, they miss faith-strengthening encouragement and examples from others who could have poured into their lives.

Scripture says that the closer we get to the day of Jesus's coming, the more dedicated we should be to meeting with other believers.

> And let us consider how to stir up one another to love and good works, not neglecting to meet together, as is the habit of some, but encouraging one another, and all the more as you see the Day drawing near. (Heb. 10:24–25 ESV)

Rather than let our teens decide for themselves whether or not to attend church, let's help them embrace the importance of being there.

WHAT TO SAY

Start with a positive . . . a compliment. Find something your teen is doing right or did well this past week. Some area where they followed Scripture really, really well, even if they weren't aware of it. Start *there*.

"I love how you _____. I'm really proud of you for that." The more specific you are, the more effective.

"In that same spirit, there's something I'd like you to work on."

I'd pause for a moment here. The tiny hesitation shows it's important, and that you want to get this right. It also gives you a chance to see how your teen is reacting—and to shoot up one more silent prayer.

"I want you to come to church with me, but without me feeling like I have to fight to get you there. What is it about going to church that bothers you, deep down?"

- If they say they can't wake up early enough, steer the conversation to how they can get better sleep Saturday night.
- If they're bored, talk about that with them. If you approach church as a chance to show appreciation to God, to encourage someone whom God will put in front of you, or to grow in knowledge and dedication to him, church gets more exciting. Go in *looking* for what God wants to do in you and your teen—and in others through you.
- Is it the pastor, the youth pastor, or the youth group? Get to the bottom of this.
- Is it the music?
- Is there a problem with the friends at your church—or the lack of them?

By knowing what's holding your teen back, you can steer the conversation in the right direction. If the thing is serious, and not something you can fix, it may be time to think about being willing to look for a new church. Carefully talk about the reasons your family might leave a church. Sometimes, it makes sense that parents leave a church—even though it meets *your* needs—to find one that better meets the needs of your *teen*.

But be cautious. You don't want to foster a consumer mentality. You also don't want them to become a church-hopper, which often leads to missed opportunities to serve, to minister to others, and to grow personally. If changing churches seems like the best choice, you'd definitely want them to join the hunt. As long as the doctrine is right, why not go to the church where *they* feel comfortable?

Getting your teen into a church they enjoy attending is infinitely more important than whatever it is that's keeping you at your current church. They also learn the life lesson that if you don't connect with a church, you don't have the option of just not attending. You find a new church—and get involved.

Now, imagine that their reasons for not attending don't warrant finding a new church. Keep the conversation going.

"I'd like you to make a new effort to attend church. Can I tell you the crazy reasons why?"

Moving into a question like this is important, I think. Before they have a chance to protest the idea of going to church—or to claim you're overreacting—you're offering to let them in on a little secret.

"Going to church is a massive win for you, and it does some things for you that I can't."

1. "It's a chance for others to encourage you in your walk with the Lord. That helps keep you on the right paths—and off the wrong ones. So, you'll get stronger, and you'll likely save yourself from some massive regrets. That's a huge win."

2. "It's a chance for you to encourage others to stay on the right paths too. Sometimes you can accomplish that in ways nobody else can. Maybe just the fact that others see you there will do that. Encouraging others to stay on the right paths? That's called obeying Almighty God. That's another win for you."

3. "It's a chance for the Holy Spirit to speak to you through the worship music and the sermon. God has laid things on their hearts all week to share with the church . . . things the church needs. That's a win I'd hate for you to miss."

4. "When you come to church without making it hard on me and without complaining? That's a massive way to honor Mom and Dad. And in Ephesians 6:1–3, God

promises that life goes better for those who honor their parents, right? That's a massive win for you."

Alternate Way to Say This

I (Tim) really love the above approach—especially as you go over that list of "wins" above. Another approach that complements this is the easy but powerful object lesson "Easy Target," which is included for your use in appendix C.

When to Say This

Pick the best possible time to do this. Take them out for dinner, make their favorite treat, whatever. Find a time when they're in a good mood—and you are too. That's when you want to hit this. At the very latest, you'd have this talk with them on Saturday night.

This *isn't* a scenario to tackle on Sunday morning, especially when you're emotionally charged with frustration on the topic—or they are. You want them to change their attitude about Sundays, and that won't happen if this turns into an argument. The truth is, they need to gather with other believers for their *own* spiritual health. So, you want to get this right. Getting them to go to church isn't enough. You want them to *want* to go to church.

Here's what you might do on Sunday morning, though. Let's say you've talked everything through with your teen. Now, this first Sunday where you're expecting them to come to church with you without complaining, get up early enough to make a great breakfast for them. There's nothing like the smell of bacon to help a teen out of bed!

Or you might announce on Saturday that the family is going out for breakfast Sunday morning, or at least for donuts. You'll leave for church earlier than normal. There's something about going out for breakfast that makes it easier for teens to roll out of bed, especially if they get to order whatever they want. And when it's time to leave the restaurant and head to church, there's no reason for them to push back like they might if they were at home.

When to Follow Up

If your teen did great that first Sunday after your talk, the car ride home from church is a great time to follow up. You want to show some excitement and gratitude.

Later in the week, make their favorite treat just to reinforce how they honored you—and that you appreciate that. And you may find that making that breakfast or going out for breakfast on Sunday mornings needs to be a regular thing.

If your teen *didn't* cooperate well, follow up before the next Sunday. You're not looking to shame or guilt them, but you have to be honest. If they don't attend, or they do it begrudgingly, they're missing those four big benefits/wins mentioned earlier. If that is the case, you might open up with your teen.

"Something scared me this week." If you tell them you're disappointed or upset with them, they'll naturally go into defense mode. But teens don't like seeing parents scared. And if my teen gave me a hard time about church after the talk I had with them? That absolutely *would* scare me! God certainly isn't going to bless our teens for failing to honor us as parents. Oh yeah . . . that *definitely* scares me!

But, if after all this, your teen still fights going to church, do you force them? That's the big question. I'll share my opinion: *Yes.* Attending church would not be optional.

I wouldn't recommend you lead with this, and I'd use a tone that was way more loving than authoritative. But Scripture commands us to meet with other believers in Hebrews 10:24–25, and I don't think parents can sit back and take an "Aw, shucks, I guess my hands are tied" attitude.

If my teen was consuming a dangerous substance, I wouldn't helplessly shrug my shoulders. I'd do *something*. So would you. We need to tackle the church issue with the same passion. For teens to push back against God's influence in their lives right when they are making so many life decisions is a lot more dangerous than substance abuse. The choices they make may have eternal consequences.

I'd get creative, for sure. I'd try everything positive I could, including the things mentioned above. I'd also tighten the leash, if I had to. If my teen can't make it to church on Sunday, I may pull back on letting them use the car on Saturday. The negative things are a last resort. There are sooo many positive things we can do. Let's pray for wisdom.

If we push our teens to go to church, do we increase the risk of losing them? The truth is, if they push back and won't go to church, they're rebelling against their parents—and God. It makes no sense to sit back for fear of losing them. They're already gone. This is a rescue mission now. This is an attempt to expose them to God's Word and God's people in the hope and with prayer that they'll be called back to him. We won't have the ability to do this after they leave our homes.

YOUR TEEN QUESTIONS IF YOU HAVE THE RIGHT RELIGION

It all happened so fast, I (Mark) didn't have time to react. During a recent drive with my family, my oldest child took over the aux and started playing her own music in the car. I thought what I'd picked was pretty good, but she had her own ideas. Within seconds, we went from chill coffeehouse vibes to an all-out karaoke session.

Developing our own preferences for small things like music, clothing, and hobbies is all part of growing up. But what about when our teenagers question if Christianity is true—or if it's really for them? Our teens will be faced with the decision to follow Jesus on their own or to embrace a different conviction and find a new way.

Why This Is Important

I'm guessing that at some point every teenager will wonder, *How do I know my religion is right?* Too often, parents don't realize their teens are questioning their faith, which makes this an essential conversation for us to initiate.

There is one truth and one way to be brought back into a right relationship with God. It's Jesus, as we read in John 14:6:

> Jesus answered, "I am the way and the truth and the life. No one comes to the Father except through me."

Any deviation from that route leads to deception and loss.

Our culture gives the opposite message to teens. "One way" and "one truth" are considered highly offensive, unloving, and arrogant. The world's message goes something like this: "You pick your way according to your own truth . . . to find your best life." This is what our teenagers hear and see every day.

When we approach this topic, it's important we understand what we're up against. The world has been telling our teens, "Any religion and belief system can be true, as long as it fits with your desires and makes you happy." In a way, those who follow this path are deceived into thinking they can become their own god. Their belief system will tend to be less about facts and truth and more about what feels right for them in this moment.

If our teenagers never establish Jesus as the only way, they'll never fully commit as followers of Jesus. This conversation is foundational—with eternal consequences. It's part of them counting the cost as they decide whether they'll personally make Jesus their only way and their absolute truth.

WHAT TO SAY

"What causes you to wonder if Christianity is the right religion?" There are so many different reasons why they might be struggling to commit to Christianity as the only way. Asking this question helps you get a clear picture of where they're at and how to best aim this conversation. Often your teen will focus on one of two areas.

1. *The facts of Christianity.* They may have doubts about the accuracy of the Bible or if Jesus really lived, died, and rose from the dead. Handling these issues is a journey. They didn't just wake up with these doubts, so realize it will be a long process to work through it all. Your focus, especially for the first conversation, is to patiently listen and ask follow-up questions. As you do, you'll better understand the core of their doubts. It also helps them organize their own thoughts. The key is you aren't debating, fighting, minimizing, or belittling. That won't lead anywhere productive.

   Likely you've grappled with your own doubts—and may even be going through a season of doubt right now. Doubts will come and go, and they can lead us to dig deeper and find answers. Be sure you're doing that. Your teen needs to see the confidence and assurance you have.

2. *How culture sees Christianity.* Your teen is caught up in the world's reasoning: *How can Christianity claim to be the only way?* If I had to bet, I'd guess this is where most teens struggle today. They might like a lot of what Jesus teaches. They just don't see Jesus as the *only* way. Life turns into a spiritual buffet of sorts. They take a little of Jesus and a little of that other faith and a side of their own philosophy and view of the world. With

that mindset, it's impossible for our teenagers to love God with all their heart and with all their soul and with all their mind (see Matt. 22:37). While they might not be entirely rejecting Jesus, a view like this doesn't allow for them to follow Jesus fully or even minimally.

"Can you think of things in the world—outside of faith or religion—that cannot both be true at the same time?" Give an example or two to start off, like traffic laws. If some drivers believe a red light means "stop," and others "go," there would be absolute chaos on the roadways. A red light cannot mean both stop *and* go. It's not open for debate. We have the law, and that truth is for *everyone to live by*.

Be creative and have some fun here. Shift to examples of natural laws that can't be changed, like we can't jump off a bridge and expect to gently float down to the ground. There's a natural law called gravity that doesn't change. It isn't an open conversation. We live in a world with truth that isn't based on our feelings or our own philosophies.

"If the world operates in truth and laws that don't change, is it possible for the same to be true of Christianity?" If your teen follows the cultural narrative, here's where they'll wrestle. To them, it sounds so unloving that other faiths lead to hell.

"It's not unloving to believe that there is only one way." You can give a quick callback to your earlier examples: It's not unloving to establish that a red light means "stop," because that actually helps people get to where they need to go more quickly and safely.

**"The same principle applies to there being only one truth in regard to faith. God established one way. He did that out of love. If God was less specific, and there were a dozen ways to heaven, how would anyone ever know for sure they were on the right path? When God established one clearly marked way, it was an act of mercy. Anyone can come and find the Truth who heals the broken, reconciles the lost, and gives a hope and future to those who had none before. Following the Truth leads to our own good and safety as we navigate the roads of life."

This part is so huge, it deserves its own analogy. "Let's say you ingested an absolutely lethal dose of poison. Your time is short, but I have the antidote. Would it be loving for me to say, 'Try what you think is best. You choose your own truth. Choose literally anything you want, and that will bring you life'? That would be so unloving! The reality is, while there are lots of things you could try, there is only one thing that will save you from death. It's the same with our sin. We could create a ton of fun ways to get through life to make us happy or feel good, but nothing or nobody other than Jesus can save us from the death penalty we face for our sin. God gave us the Truth, the antidote, as the one way to reach him so that we can be saved. We just need to swallow it."

Alternate Way to Say This

This is a great opportunity to use the Ask the Expert approach from appendix A. Is there someone your teenager knows and respects who has either had these same questions before or is super passionate about these issues and has put a lot of time and thought into them? Would they be willing to talk through these questions on a deeper level with your teen?

There are amazing podcasts and books out there by experts. For example, Jonathan Pokluda gave a helpful sermon at Passion Conference 2024.* Check it out online with your teen.

Another alternate idea would be the Object Lesson approach in appendix A, or check out "The Right Combination" in *The Very Best, Hands-On, Kinda Dangerous Family Devotions*, vol. 1.

---

*"Passion 2024 Talks: The Way, The Truth, and the Life—Jonathan Pokluda," Passion Conferences, January 14, 2024, https://passionconferences.com/message/the-way-the-truth-and-the-life-jonathan-pokluda/.

When to Say This

This is a great topic for a walk and talk. I know, it sounds oddly specific to say you should take a walk for this conversation, but let me explain.

Walking is a great help to the brain, for a lot of reasons, but one relevant for this chapter is how it aids us in processing and organizing our thoughts. Part of what your teenager needs here is to sift through all the messages in their head and beliefs that have built up over time. This is a lot to process!

When to Follow Up

Try following up within a few days. If you sense frustration or defensiveness, it's fine to temporarily step back. You can remind them, "I was really thankful for our conversation the other day, and I care about you and how you're processing this. I know you might need more time, but I do want to make sure we can talk about it again soon. I'll check back with you in a couple of weeks."

YOUR TEEN IS QUESTIONING THE TRUTH OF GOD'S WORD

I (Mark) have a rule I live by: *Don't trust anything you see on the internet.* Nothing. Unfortunately, I've adopted this rule due to some embarrassing lessons. Too many times I've fallen for a fake article or doctored photo. I once believed that A-list movie star Matthew McConaughey was moving to the no-name suburb I grew up in. I wish I was kidding.

Photos can be altered in every imaginable way. We doubt the very images we see with our eyes. Someone writing an article may be less focused on getting the facts right than the number of clicks it will receive. We may have grown up believing all news sources reported the truth, but now we know better. Accuracy is secondary today. As a result, often our first reaction is to question everything.

It's no wonder, then, why the Bible is met with such cynicism. We see it as the inspired, true words of God. But our teens often see the Bible as just another item on a long list of resources claiming to be reliable and to speak with authority. The problem is, everything else on that list has failed to live up to its own claims.

Why This Is Important

The Bible makes strong claims about itself, such as, "All Scripture is breathed out by God" (2 Tim. 3:16 ESV). That means every word found in the Bible is from God, and every verse must be true because God is unable to speak untruth. Follow me just one more layer to see why this matters. If there's just *one* part of the Bible that's proven to be untrue, it would make the entire book unreliable. The Bible would then contradict itself. This is a big deal. If any part of the Bible failed to be fully true, the very core of our faith would unravel. If our teens are questioning the truth of some part of the Bible, they're vulnerable to the enemy.

- *We don't have faith unless we truly believe.* And we can't truly believe if we don't think something is true. When the truth of Scripture cannot be accepted, salvation can't happen. You can't have one without the other. Believing Jesus is who he said he is and trusting the reliability of the account of his life is the absolute bedrock foundation to receiving the gospel. No one has saving faith without believing the Word is true. And anyone who does not believe does not possess saving faith. That's a really scary thought when it comes to our teens.
- *If the Bible isn't accepted as truth, then why would our teenagers care to apply any of its teaching to their everyday lives?* Every personal application comes from a

conviction that the Bible has authority over us. If the truth of any part of the Bible is doubted by our teens, all reasons to put it into practice disappear.
- *If our teens aren't using God's Word to guide them as their truth, they'll undoubtedly look to find direction elsewhere.* Psalm 119:105 says, "Your word is a lamp to my feet and a light to my path" (ESV). The truth of the Bible illuminates a path for us to walk that leads to new life and our ultimate good. To reject the Bible and choose anything else as true is to follow our own way down a broad path that leads to destruction.

WHAT TO SAY

"What are you having a hard time believing in the Bible?" You're listening for two things when you ask this.

1. *What specifically seems untrustworthy to them about the Bible.* You aren't interested in debating them on this, but you do want to dial in your conversation where they need it most.
2. *What/who is the source of their distrust.* It's possible the source can be discredited. But more than that, it tells you where your teenager looks for reliable information.

"There are a number of reasons why I believe every word of the Bible." You're going to give three areas of proof. If they've already expressed a specific area of doubt, start there. If not, you can walk through all three of these. Remember, you aren't arguing or debating. Right now, you're calmly sharing why *you* believe.

1. **"It has been historically affirmed as true."** There are two parts to the historical accuracy of the Bible. First,

the accuracy of the details written in the narrative. When we look at historians' accounts and archaeological discoveries, we find they all support the details of events recorded in the Old and New Testaments. Second, *the historical accuracy in the Bible's precision of translation over the years.* It's natural to wonder how we got our Bible, and why we see variances between versions. If we look at our Bible now and compare it to our earliest copies of Scripture, the consistency is amazing. The more we dig into the process of how we got our Bible, the stronger the case we can make for it being true.

2. **"The Bible proves itself to be true."** The Bible was written over a period of at least fifteen hundred years by about forty different authors from different countries and cultures. And yet all sixty-six books fit together perfectly. The details of prophecies in the Old Testament about the Messiah are seen to be true hundreds of years later in the person and work of Jesus. The message from the garden of Eden in Genesis to the garden in heaven in Revelation is consistent in that it never contradicts itself. But more than that, it all builds on itself to form one cohesive teaching about who God is and who he has created us to be.

3. **"I've experienced the Bible to be true."** It's important to share your own experiences of how the Bible has helped you. As your teenager hears specific stories of how you've experienced the truth of the Bible in your life, that's *powerful*.

"What can I do to help answer your questions?" They might find it helpful to read a book that addresses some of the questions they're facing. There are so many resources out there! Or maybe they just need to sit down with the Bible and actually read through more of it before coming to a conclusion. But whatever would be a helpful next step, offer to do it *with* them. This sets you up for future follow-ups. It also underscores that it's not you versus them. Instead, this is you *with* them, helping them find answers to life's greatest questions.

Alternate Way to Say This

I (Mark) can't think of a more powerful way to impress the truth of God's Word on our teens than by sharing how we've experienced it to be true. I'd start there, as outlined. But if you want something different when you follow up, check out the Ask the Expert approach in appendix A. A pastor should be able to help and can refer you to books and other resources.

Another option is the Field Trip approach. I haven't known one person who took a solid Christian tour of the Holy Land and hasn't come back more convinced than ever of the absolute truth of God's Word. Expensive . . . yes. But if that's what it takes to open our teens' eyes to the truth, it's worth it. That will benefit them for their entire life—and for eternity. So many parents are quick to help pay for college, a place where so many kids walk away from their faith. A Holy Land trip might be a monumentally *better* investment.

When to Say This

You really want to have this talk at a time and place where you won't be interrupted. To me, this feels like a perfect bonfire conversation. A fire provides a comfortable atmosphere and somehow encourages teens to be totally open. It also doesn't feel rushed, making it easier to give enough space for the full discussion. This is important. If you can't make it happen around a fire, find another setting with similar qualities.

When to Follow Up

The day after you have your conversation, give your teen some positive feedback. Something like, **"Thanks for that conversation last night. I really appreciate you opening up."** It's important that your teenager knows you're with them as they wrestle through their doubts.

A more thorough follow-up can happen within a few weeks. **"Have you thought more about our conversation about the Bible being fully true?"** or **"We talked about the Bible being true. Where are you at with that now? Anything new?"** This will be a process for them, one that will benefit from regular check-ins and a series of follow-up conversations after this initial one.

YOUR TEEN WONDERS HOW GOD CAN ALLOW BAD THINGS TO HAPPEN

Unless we address this issue before our teens leave home, they're vulnerable to an enemy deception. That's a scary thought! Together, let's arm and protect them with truth.

Why This Is Important

If we fail to help our teens see how God is truly good—even when bad things happen—the enemy uses that to plant seeds of doubt.

- *How can God be good if he allows this?*
- *How can we believe he cares when innocent people/kids get hurt?*

The enemy knows this seed of doubt can grow a mighty tree. He'll use that tree as a battering ram against our teens' faith, turning them from God.

WHAT TO SAY

Instead of only focusing on helping your teen, also show how they can help their friends. That may intrigue them a bit more to listen.

"There's something you'll wrestle with—or a friend will. Anyone who hasn't processed this issue well will be vulnerable to the enemy. Let's talk about that so you'll be protected, and you can protect your friends."

Remember, you're coming alongside your teen here to debunk an enemy lie. If you come across as "preachy," you'll lose them.

"How can a good God allow bad things to happen in this world, like natural disasters, injustice, sickness, and death?"

Now, this next point is a biggie. Your teen probably hasn't considered this. Let them process it for a few minutes.

"First of all, this isn't really God's world. I mean technically, it is. But it's sort of loaned out right now—to Satan."

Read them these Bible verses from when Satan was tempting Jesus.

> Again, the devil took him to a very high mountain and showed him all the kingdoms of the world and their splendor. "All this I will give you," he said, "if you will bow down and worship me." (Matt. 4:8–9)

The devil reigned over the kingdoms of this world *and still does*. He was willing to share his kingdom with Jesus—if Jesus would turn from God. Although God created all and rules over all, he has loaned earth to Satan for a time. Ever since the fall of humankind in the garden of Eden, we've seen the devil's dominating influence over the entire world.

> I will not say much more to you, for the prince of this world is coming. He has no hold over me. (John 14:30)

"Jesus refers to the devil as the 'prince of this world.' For the moment, this world is Satan's. So, when we see injustice and tragedy and sickness and horrible things happening, we can remember that's exactly what happens in a sinful world under the rule of a corrupt, uncaring leader. That leader is Satan—not God.

Even if God has loaned the world to the devil, can't he step in and make things right? Sure—and he often does. But not always. Why?"

Here are four points of truth and logic that will help explain that.

1. "When sin entered the world, sickness, death, and all manner of evil came with it. And because God *is* good, and he *does* care, he did something about it." He sent his Son to rescue us from sin, right? Even now, if God didn't allow evil to remain on earth, people would not feel they needed a Savior—and would miss being saved. So God, in his great love for us, allows evil to remain until all who are going to be saved actually are. Second Peter 3:9 reads,

    > The Lord is not slow in keeping his promise, as some understand slowness. Instead he is patient with you, not wanting anyone to perish, but everyone to come to repentance.

2. "God often allows bad things to happen to protect us . . . to keep us from making mistakes that hurt us." Bad things often cause us to rethink where we're headed in life, prompting us to seek God and change direction. Think of a personal example to share.

3. "God often allows bad things to happen so that we stick closer to him for our own well-being." The enemy

has an easier time picking off strays—or those who fall behind.

4. **"God often allows bad things to happen so that he can shine through us in ways he never could otherwise."** When bad things drive us to God, his power, peace, joy, and so forth are displayed in our lives. Our relationship with him is strengthened, and we're better able to help and witness to others.

Alternate Way to Say This

The Field Trip approach from appendix A could work nicely. Imagine taking your teen to a building that leases office space. Look at the list of business tenants together. Each company is responsible for how they run their business—not the landlord. That would lead right into showing how the devil is like a tenant in this world with a temporary lease. The Object Lesson approach is another alternate way to say this, or check out "How Can a Good God Allow This?" from *The Very Best, Hands-On, Kinda Dangerous Family Devotions*, vol. 3.

When to Say This

Teens are ripe for this talk anytime there's a world disaster, they are hit with bad news, or their family/friends face hard times or tragedy. But even if everything is going well right now, you must schedule this talk. Pick a day in the next week. Create a relaxed atmosphere. Order a pizza or make their favorite treat. Make it fun!

When to Follow Up

Anytime our kids are concerned about something bad that happened is a great time to remind them that the devil is a temporary tenant of this world. God, in his great love and mercy, provided a rescue for all who put their faith in Jesus. Maybe read this passage.

> As for you, **you were dead** in your transgressions and sins, in which you used to live **when you followed the ways of this world and of the ruler of the kingdom of the air,** the spirit who is now at work in those who are disobedient. All of us also lived among them at one time, gratifying the cravings of our flesh and following its desires and thoughts. Like the rest, we were by nature deserving of wrath. **But because of his great love for us, God, who is rich in mercy, made us alive with Christ even when we were dead in transgressions—it is by grace you have been saved.** And God raised us up with Christ and seated us with him in the heavenly realms in Christ Jesus, in order that in the coming ages he might show the incomparable riches of his grace, expressed in his kindness to us in Christ Jesus. (Eph. 2:1–7, emphasis added)

Mom and Dad, you're finding creative ways to give your teen truth—something God created you to do. Keep up the good work!

CONCERNS YOUR TEEN ISN'T GROWING IN THEIR FAITH/SPENDING TIME IN THE WORD

Teaching is a big part of parenting. Think about it: You've taught your kids so much! How to tie their shoes, ride a bike, throw a ball, and roast the perfect s'more.

As they get older, the list of essentials to teach changes. Hygiene. Driving. But when it comes to teaching our teens how to grow in their faith, oftentimes parents step back. But our teens need us to step up now more than ever.

Why This Is Important

These next years for our teenagers are filled with life-altering decisions. College. Career. New friendships. Often choosing a spouse for life.

- We want them to approach all these big life moments with a strong foundation in God and what it means to live for him.
- We want these decisions made with God's help and direction.

If they aren't growing in their faith, these won't happen, which results in tragic mistakes with lifetime consequences. And if our teens don't learn to prioritize time with God while they're with Mom and Dad, it won't easily happen later.

As if that wasn't enough, Satan is described in 1 Peter 5:8 as our adversary who "prowls around like a roaring lion, seeking someone to devour" (ESV). Too often Satan gets a foothold in our teens during these critical years. If our teens aren't growing in their faith, they're vulnerable to his schemes to distract and destroy.

WHAT TO SAY

The key to spiritual growth and becoming more like Jesus isn't a secret. It's spending time with God—and putting what we learn into practice. If you don't see fruit and evidence of growth and godliness in your teenager's life, it's a result of *not* spending time with him. John 15 speaks pretty clearly to that.

Most teenagers give the same two excuses for why they don't spend time with God.

1. They don't have time.
2. They don't know *how* to spend time with God. Even if a student has grown up in the church, it's common

for them to feel discouraged, distracted, and confused about reading the Bible and praying.

Teaching your teen how to do this is your main focus here. *This means showing them how to prioritize spending time with God and helping them discover the process and approach to doing so that will be helpful for them.*

"Tomorrow, I want you to meet me at (<u>6:00 a.m.</u>) at (<u>my desk</u>). Bring your Bible." You want to start this conversation by inviting them to the place where *you* meet with God. Customize that time and location based on your practice.

You might get pushback about how early it is, but that's part of the power of this meeting.

"I invited you here to see the most important moments of my day. Yeah, it's early. It used to be a struggle for me to be here as well. But I've found it to be so worthwhile that I can't miss this time for anything." There is added weight to your words when your teenager experiences this early-morning moment. They'll hear how quiet the house is. They'll feel their tired mind trying to wake up. This is part of showing the priority and power of spending time with God. You're inviting them into your space, and hopefully they'll feel the honor of that. They'll also get to see how you do it, which gives them a good starting point for their own time with God.

Quick sidenote: Teenagers living in the same house as us have a front-row seat to view our walk with God. They see our daily habits. How we prioritize time with God and make decisions in ways that honor God. This is one of the most beneficial forms of discipleship our kids will ever have. These years are crucial because they're our last years to model our relationship with God to our kids in such close proximity.

"First Timothy 4 calls on us to train for godliness. This is how I train. It isn't easy. It requires sacrifice."

Share how you've seen God use this time in your life and when it has helped you through anxiety, uncertainty, or grief.

"If you want God to change you and use you? If you want to know God more? Realize it won't just happen. You'll need to train."

Is your teen involved in sports, music, drama, debate team—or maybe striving to be on the honor roll? Ask them what kind of dedication or training that takes. Clearly, they already know how to sacrifice and put in the hard work. They know how to train! Now you can encourage them to use those same kinds of skills to deepen their relationship with God.

Here's a few reminders about this time you spend with them.

- Show them what you do in your time with God. Have them read the same Scripture passage you read and ask them if they found anything confusing. Was there anything that stood out?
- Don't dig deep just to impress them, or they'll think they can't study Scripture on their own. Take every opportunity to encourage them: "That's such a great question." "Wow, super good observation."
- Keep the time short. You want them to see this as attainable.
- Make it enjoyable. You want them to feel inspired to try it on their own.
- Realize doing this once won't be enough.

"Let's meet back here tomorrow at 6:00 a.m." When you meet, put in some creative effort to help them enjoy the time. Maybe bring donuts and fresh juice or coffee.

After a few days of doing this routine together, move to the next step.

"Starting tomorrow, I want you to pick a time and place that works for you." It's important they start doing this on their own. Allow them the freedom to customize their time with God in ways they feel comfortable or excited to try.

Alternate Way to Say This

Check out the Field Trip approach in appendix A. This would be a great choice if you normally have your time with God at a coffee shop, breakfast restaurant, or park somewhere. Taking your teen to the very spot where you meet with God is powerful.

A second option? The Shameless Bribe approach, as long as you're careful. **"I want to challenge you to have time with God daily—for one month. When that time is up, if you can honestly say it wasn't worth it, I'll give you $100."** You're not paying them to have time with God but offering to pay if they don't see any payoff. And if your teen says it wasn't worth it, you know you have more work to do, right?

When to Say This

Don't initiate this conversation on the heels of a fight or a big mess-up on their part. That will only frame this conversation as focusing on behavioral change, which is not what you're after. You want *heart* change. And you don't want your teen thinking of time with God as a punishment.

Instead, find a time when they have some momentum. After a retreat, following a week at camp, after they're baptized, or on the heels of a sermon that moved them. Initiating the conversation then will be more natural.

A mile-marker event also works. New Year's. A birthday. **"Now that you're fifteen, I want to teach you something that's made a huge difference in my life."**

When to Follow Up

Your teen will need your encouragement and coaching if they're going to find long-term success in this.

"It's been two weeks since you started having time with God on your own. What are you seeing is working? What has been

difficult?" This time of circling back will provide another chance to encourage their progress—and also help solve problems that are sure to pop up.

CONCERNS YOUR TEEN ISN'T BEING KIND, LOVING, OR DEMONSTRATING FRUIT OF THE SPIRIT

As parents, we want our kids to grow more loving. More kind. In this chaotic and confusing world, we desire them to possess that deep peace only God can give. We want them to be strong and to develop a high level of self-control too . . . saying no when that is best and right. We want them to be patient with others. And we want them to be dependably trustworthy—or, said another way, *faithful*. To family. And most definitely to God.

Much of what we've just described are character qualities the Holy Spirit grows in his kids if they let him.

Why This Is Important

Love, joy, peace, forbearance, kindness, goodness, faithfulness, gentleness, and self-control: The presence of the fruit of the Spirit in someone's life—in increasing amounts—is a huge indicator of their true relationship with the Lord.

If we aren't seeing this fruit in our teens but instead are seeing the deeds of the flesh mentioned in Galatians 5:19–21, we're left with one of two conclusions.

1. Their relationship with the Lord isn't genuine.
2. They're resisting the Holy Spirit.

Both are scary thoughts!

WHAT TO SAY

You don't want your teen making excuses, getting defensive, or blame-shifting, which may happen if you simply point out examples of how they don't exhibit fruit of the Spirit. This is about your teen coming face-to-face with who they really are.

Start with something entirely nonthreatening.

"**What if a farmer planted the finest apple trees in the world, and the orchard got plenty of sunshine and rain, but the fruit was sparse—or nonexistent? What would you conclude?**"

You can work with whatever your teen gives you, even if they simply shrug and don't say a word. You just want to emphasize a couple of things.

"**If the farmer did their part right and there was adequate rain and sunshine, we'd guess there might be a problem with the soil. There's a parallel to life here. God is like a farmer. If we're truly following Jesus, he's planted his Holy Spirit in us to grow us more like him.**"

Read these verses, holding the Bible so they can see the verses for themself.

> **But the fruit of the Spirit is love, joy, peace, forbearance, kindness, goodness, faithfulness, gentleness and self-control. Against such things there is no law. Those who belong to Christ Jesus have crucified the flesh with its passions and desires. Since we live by the Spirit, let us keep in step with the Spirit. (Gal. 5:22–25)**

"**These are the kinds of things we want coming out of our lives, don't you think?**"

It's important to let your teen come up with an answer—even if it's only in their head. Hopefully, the Spirit is working on them right now, building a longing in them for these treasures that money can't buy.

"So, what is coming out of the soil of your life? What are you seeing?"

Give them a moment to reflect.

"As Christians, if our lives aren't producing crops of love and joy and kindness and goodness and peace and so on, what could that mean? Maybe one of a couple of things?"

Give them a chance to come up with an answer. If you have a personal story of a time when you didn't produce good fruit or an example of when you resisted the Spirit, this would be a great time to share that. It will help your kid to see you being vulnerable and honest. Likely, at this moment in the conversation, they're thinking of times you failed rather than times *they* failed. So, you're putting that on the table by talking about your bad fruit and what you've learned. Then you need to move on and get them thinking about *their* life.

"If we aren't growing more loving, kind, patient, and self-controlled, either we've never really surrendered our life to God or we're resisting the work of the Holy Spirit in our lives. Both are scary." Then read these verses together:

> Examine yourselves to see whether you are in the faith; test yourselves. Do you not realize that Christ Jesus is in you—unless, of course, you fail the test? (2 Cor. 13:5)

> Do not quench the Spirit. (1 Thess. 5:19)

"What about you? If you aren't seeing increasing amounts of good fruit in your life, is it because you don't have the Spirit or because you're fighting what the Spirit wants to do in your life? Are you cutting off regular doses of the water and light of the Word that you need if you want to grow?"

Okay, these are tough, tough questions. But can you think of more important questions to ask at this point in your teen's life? Sometimes they need to examine themselves: *Am I really a follower, or am I resisting God's Holy Spirit in some way?*

The big question now: Do they want this situation to change, and if so, what would be their next step? Help them come up with the answers to this. This is a moment for them to search their soul. That isn't something you can do for them—and help them understand this isn't something they're to try accomplishing on their own, either. Do they see they lack patience? Simply "trying harder" to be patient doesn't work. Patience is a fruit produced by the work of the Holy Spirit. Our teens, like us, need to surrender to God and ask the Holy Spirit to grow this seed in their lives.

Alternate Way to Say This

The Let Me Tell You a Story approach from appendix A could work well if you share a personal example of how you quenched the Spirit—and the price you paid or lesson you learned. The Handoff approach is equally valid if you think your teen would handle the conversation better if it were with someone else. The Field Trip approach could be effective too. Taking your teen to a farmer's field or orchard would be a great way to open this conversation and help the points you make truly stick with them.

When to Say This

Unless you're using the Field Trip approach, try to have this conversation at night. Talking around a campfire or even sitting on the edge of your teen's bed works. Often, teens open up better in the dark.

If you're seeing behavior, attitudes, or choices that are inconsistent with a Christian life, you need to have this conversation really soon.

When to Follow Up

Early. Often. Honestly? Most of the time you'll follow up in prayer with the Lord. And sometimes with your teen too. If you see good fruit, you may want to comment on it.

"When I saw how you reacted to _____, I found myself thanking God for that good fruit the Spirit was growing in your life. Keep surrendering to him—and keep that going."

Confronting teens with their failures is rarely effective. A better approach? Call yourself out when you've failed.

"Did you hear how I just talked to Mom? That wasn't kind or patient. That's an example of me resisting the Spirit instead of surrendering. I'm sorry about that poor example. I'll be praying that I'll do better."

Then you have to work on it—with the help of the Holy Spirit. This openness on your part can make a lasting difference in the life of your teen.

PERSONAL HABITS AND BEHAVIOR

BEING RESPONSIBLE AND PRODUCTIVE WITH THEIR FREE TIME

Part of our job as parents is to train our teens how to be responsible, productive adults. Helping them think through how much "free time" they have—and what they do with it—is an important part of that.

Why This Is Important

As parents, we're to be preparing our kids for life as adults. Scott Ziegler, lead pastor of The Bridge Community Church in the Chicago area, says something like this: "As parents, we're raising adults, not kids." It makes sense, right? We want our teens to succeed at whatever God has for them in life. They'll need to develop some self-discipline if they're going to do that. Learning how to use their free time wisely is a good place to start.

If we don't help our teens with direction in these areas, they'll tend to squander their free time instead of becoming all God has planned for them. They can develop a habit of being lazy, which won't do them any favors in the long run. Two Scripture verses come to mind:

> Diligent hands will rule,
> but laziness ends in forced labor. (Prov. 12:24)

> Through laziness, the rafters sag;
> because of idle hands, the house leaks. (Eccles. 10:18)

Laziness ends in unrealized potential and becomes its own kind of slavery. Laziness leads to loss. And if our teens view their free time as solely "theirs," they'll miss the truth that life is a gift from God—and he has some plans for us. God is our boss, right? Without that understanding, our teens are apt to spend too much of their free time on things with no real value for their future as adults, much less eternity.

WHAT TO SAY

Start with something positive . . . a compliment.

"**You're getting older. Sometimes I can hardly believe how fast you're growing up.**"

Next, make a clarifying statement.

"**You know my job is to help prepare you for adult life, right? With that in mind, I think you're ready for us to step your training up to the next level.**"

If you approach this in a positive way, your teen is much less likely to push back.

"**We need to work on how much free time you have and what you do with it. What are some things you'd like to accomplish or goals you might have?**"

It might be something they want to learn. A skill to sharpen. A chance to earn some money with a job.

"**Another thing to think about is how you'll use a portion of this free time to regularly help the family.**" Are there regular chores they can do around the house on a daily or weekly basis? Mowing the lawn. Lending a hand doing dishes. Helping a younger sibling with homework. Doing laundry. Make a list together of ways they can be a consistent contributor to the family.

"**God also teaches us to think about others. So, let's think of some ways we can use some of our time to help those outside our immediate family.**"

Could they be helping a neighbor? A grandparent? It's important that your teen learns to look beyond themselves.

"**There are also some life skills I want to be sure you learn to do well. Let's make a list of these. What types of things would you like to be sure you learn?**"

You'll have things you want your teen to know before they leave the nest, but be sure to get their input too. Here are some ideas to get you thinking.

- Cooking basic meals.
- Checking tire pressure. Changing a tire. Scheduling car maintenance.
- Painting a room or a shed, fence, and so on.
- Performing home maintenance: vacuuming, washing floors, changing furnace filters.
- Doing laundry: sorting, washing, drying, folding, putting away.
- Developing and sticking with a budget.
- Getting a job and learning a great work ethic.
- Managing their time and being a self-starter without needing reminders.

- Setting goals: Daily. Weekly. Monthly. Yearly. This should include doing things for the family or others, too, not just for themselves.

"Let's set up a punch list of these things we've talked about. Things to learn and things to do with free time." By doing this, you'll also help them develop that time management skill. Be sure this list is in writing and you have a copy of it. Your teen's copy ought to be posted in a place where they'll see it often.

Then help them break it down so they learn to develop those daily, weekly, and monthly to-do lists.

Alternate Way to Say This

Look at different strategies in appendix A. The Object Lesson approach can work well here. Check out "Time to Burn" and "Food Frenzy" in *The Very Best, Hands-On, Kinda Dangerous Family Devotions*, vol. 3.

When to Say This

Honestly, the younger your teen is for this one, the better. Helping a young teen use their free time well is a really good thing. It would be especially important to have this conversation a few weeks before the school season is over for summer. Otherwise, your teen may do a lot more sleeping late or get sucked into more screen time than is good for them.

Ideally, for this talk, get your teen off by themselves—perhaps to a fast-food restaurant. Order them a snack. A treat. And talk to them like an adult. If you talk down to them, *everything* backfires. Who likes being talked down to?

When to Follow Up

Circle back with them on this regularly. Do so every few days at first, or maybe weekly. Review their to-do lists. How did they do? When they've accomplished something on it without needed reminders, that's huge! Celebrate with them. Encourage them. When they check off something *really* big on the list, celebrate in a big way. Take them to a ball game, a play, a climbing wall, out for ice cream, whatever they'd be really interested in.

And you'll need to actively create opportunities to tackle those things on their list that *you* need to teach them. "Hey, son/daughter, how about we check something off your list? Are you ready to learn how to change a tire?" The same goes for budgeting, and so forth.

If you're going to the store to pick up supplies for some project, bring your teen with and show them what you're doing . . . how you're thinking things through.

If you're making a big purchase, like buying a car, bring them with so they can experience that—and gain more life skills in the process.

When we help our teens be wise about how they use their free time and the abilities God has given them, we'll have a better atmosphere around the house—and we'll be preparing them to be more responsible adults too.

TEXTING VERSUS REAL CONVERSATIONS

We are the first generation of parents in the history of the world to deal with the texting habits of our teenagers. In a way, that makes us pioneers, exploring the unknown and carving new trails. Historically, being a trailblazing pioneer has been anything but easy. That's not much different today—especially if the trail we're blazing leads to changing how our teens use their phones.

Why This Is Important

Good communication is a key to better friendships, better job performance, better marriages, better parenting, and much more. We all agree with that. Poor communication leads to problems. Trouble. Unnecessary pain.

Naturally, we want all those "better" things for our kids . . . the things that come from good communication. The trouble is, texting is just about the poorest form of communication there is.

- We can't watch body language to help us get the full picture of what someone is saying or thinking.
- We can't look into the eyes of the speaker to help discern what is being said or not said.
- We don't hear their tone of voice or see their facial expression, which leads to misunderstandings.
- We often text short, abbreviated messages without bothering to proofread them. They contain autocorrected words, misspellings, or missing punctuation, skyrocketing the chance for confusion or misunderstandings.
- Many people scan texts quickly, in multitasking mode, which leads to them missing part of what the sender expected them to get.

When our kids are texting, likely they're not communicating in the most effective way at that moment. And they're not developing their communication skills either. They're not learning to read eyes, body language, tone of voice, and so on. All these things take practice. If our teens are going to reap the full benefits and rewards of good communication, they'll need to use texting a lot less than they do.

Note: If we as parents are texting when we should be talking, we'll have a monumentally harder time getting through to our kids on this topic. Let's work on this ourselves too. Personally, if

I (Tim) have good news, I usually resist the urge to text it to my wife. Texting is a weak form of communication, and I'd rather tell my wife good news in a stronger way. I'm going to tell her in person so I can see her face, so she can hear my tone, and so we can celebrate together. That builds something between us far more bonding and significant than if I'd shared that news via text—and gotten a happy face emoji back.

WHAT TO SAY

Start with a question that might intrigue your teen.

"What if I said that you would do better with friendships, distinguish yourself in any job situation, and certainly score points with the opposite sex in a dating relationship simply by changing one habit?"

They'll doubtlessly be suspicious, but they'll want to know.

"Text less. Talk more. That's it. That's your key to greater success whenever it comes to dealing with people."

This would be the time to talk about that a bit. Can you share times you've misunderstood someone because of a text—or someone misunderstood you? Maybe your teen will have an example to share too.

"What makes texting not nearly as strong a way to communicate as actually talking to someone?"

Get their input. Likely you'll want to cover that list of things mentioned in the "Why This Is Important" section above. Any one of those can lead to miscommunication.

Now mention one other massive shortcoming of texting.

"Texting often compounds our problems because it reduces our awareness of what's around us at the moment. We see people texting while driving, walking, crossing the street, and sitting across the table from family or friends. Those texting may truly believe they are engaged with those around them, but it's obvious to anyone watching just how much they're missing.

Texting can cause problems and rob us of the benefits of better communication. How can we set ourselves up to do better with this?"

If your teen seems to be open to this, you have the conversation in a terrific spot. Now you can brainstorm ways to break your texting habits, reduce the number of texts you send, and so forth. Do that with your teen so you are both on the same team. Brainstorming together is far more effective than simply dictating new guidelines.

"Let's text less" is easy to say, but it's difficult to measure real progress. Make a list together of specific situations. For example,

- I won't text anyone while I'm visiting with someone else. I'll focus my attention on the live person in front of me.
- I won't bring my phone into the room while I'm studying.
- I won't text something I could say in person or with a phone call within the next day or so.
- I'll avoid late-night text conversations. I'm tired. The person I'm texting is tired. This is a formula for the worst text conversations ever.
- I'll avoid firing off/answering texts at stoplights while driving.

Alternate Way to Say This

Check out the Game/Challenge approach in appendix A. Maybe even set up a family competition to see who can reduce the highest percentage of outgoing texts over the course of the next week. The prize to the winner should be something worth winning.

When to Say This

Anytime is a good time, as long as it's not when you're frustrated with your teen's phone habits. You want to go into this in a calm and wise way.

When to Follow Up

If you do the Game/Challenge approach, you'll have a built-in follow-up when the game is over. I kind of like that approach. But regardless, you need to circle back to this topic regularly. This is about establishing better habits for yourself and your kids.

A good time to circle back to this topic is over a shared meal. As you relate how *you've* been working on texting less and talking more over the past week, it will cause your teen to think about that too. If you can share a specific time you chose to talk instead of text—and it paid off in some way—that would be ideal.

Mom, Dad, let's set the pace. We know of one mom who deliberately returns a text from her kids with a phone call when possible. The point is, text less. Talk more.

YOUR TEEN IS USING LANGUAGE YOU DON'T APPROVE OF

What is "bad language"? Our first thought is usually those four-letter words. We have those all ranked in our minds . . . the bad ones and the *really* bad ones.

But this conversation isn't just about *those* words. There are myriad ways we can use our words in destructive ways. Gossip, slander, and insults fit into this discussion as well. Our teenagers need a conversation on this topic, even if they aren't the ones throwing around f-bombs.

Why This Is Important

Clearly, the tongue can cause serious damage to our lives—and to the relationships around us.

James 3:6 says, "The tongue is set among our members, staining the whole body, setting on fire the entire course of life, and set on fire by hell" (ESV). Later, verse 8 says, "It is a restless evil, full of deadly poison" (ESV).

Jesus taught us that our words are a window into our heart: "Out of the abundance of the heart his mouth speaks" (Luke 6:45 ESV).

Our words really matter. They reveal what our heart loves and is devoted to. Ephesians 4:29 says, "Let no corrupting talk come out of your mouths, but only such as is good for building up, as fits the occasion, that it may give grace to those who hear" (ESV).

The word *corrupting* means harmful or worthless. We're to avoid speaking in ways that could harm others in some way. Instead, we should choose words that benefit and bring life to others. God cares about what we say and how we use our words—which is why this topic is so important.

WHAT TO SAY

"I've noticed you saying some words that I'm uncomfortable with you using. I want to talk about it with you. Why are you using those words?" Say the words—out loud—that you hear them using. You'll get bonus points *and* gain shock value that will underscore that these words are crass. If your teen is uncomfortable with their parent saying those words, they can understand why you're uncomfortable with *them* using the words.

There are so many reasons teenagers use these words.

- They want to sound older.
- They seek to fit in.

- They are fighting back against someone who hurt them.
- They hear that language so much, using it themselves becomes more natural.
- They want to emphasize how upset they are or how strongly they feel about something at the moment.

Listen closely to their answers and resist the temptation to debate their reasoning. This isn't the time for that. That would almost certainly shut down the conversation before you've accomplished anything.

There's also a chance they get defensive here, making a case that these words are so commonly used that they aren't considered bad anymore. In many respects, they're right. But on the other hand, the music industry has been pressured to warn their audience when a song has certain words. They label it with an "E" for explicit. The film industry has adopted similar ratings. Yes, the words are commonly used in our culture, but they're still considered to be bad.

If our world sees these words as crass, we should too.

"Most words fall into two categories. Those that build up, and those that corrupt." (If you pronounce both words with a similar tone and emphasis, "BUILD up or CORE-rupt" almost rhymes, which will help them remember.)

"How do these words you're using benefit or build others up?" Give them a moment to process that. Then share Ephesians 4:29—and how it applies to their situation. If they gossip, you can help them understand what gossip is and what makes it so bad. It's corrupting. If they are swearing, explain how those words don't build others up in any way either.

"You said your reason for using these words was _____. That makes some sense. The Bible actually digs deeper. It says, 'Out of the overflow of the heart his mouth speaks.' So, whatever comes out of our mouth simply reveals what's in our heart."

You want to get to the heart because that's the root of their language. When the root is good, the fruit will also be good.

Say their initial reason for why they swear is that their friends do. That means their heart is set on pleasing people more than God. They want to fit in, which is the opposite of who God has called us to be. We're to be holy as he is. A light on a hill. Salt of the earth. *This* is the heart of the matter. This is the struggle.

"Where is it most difficult for you to avoid using bad words, or to build up others with what you say?" They'll undoubtedly have places where they're tempted to use bad language. Or they'll struggle with building up a specific person they find to be super difficult. It's good to let them express that, and it gives you specific areas to ask follow-up questions a few weeks from now.

This is also a good time to remind them that God's principles apply to our texts just as much as they do to our talk. Sometimes it's easier for teens to fall into habits of using bad words, acronyms, or harmful gossip through texts without noticing it.

"Let's practice something this week:

- Avoid the nasty, crass words we might say or text.
- Replace words that hurt or tear down with words that build up (even if we think the other person deserves tearing down).

There'll be times you slip. It won't be easy, but keep at it, and you'll be moving in the direction God wants. That's a good thing. How we talk to and about others is an indicator of where we are spiritually. And we want to be growing more and more like Jesus. If we ask God to help us with this, he will."

Alternate Way to Say This

Try the Game/Challenge approach from appendix A. Instead of making the game about *not saying* certain words, make it more positive. Set a goal for how many times they build others up (without flattery, though) during the week through talk or texts. If they reach the goal, they earn a prize. And while they're enjoying that prize, you can remind them that the outcome is always more fun when we use our words to help others instead of to harm.

When to Say This

There's something about that moment when one of those words (or a few of them) slip out. Especially when it's in front of parents. It's uncomfortable for our teens. Let's use that tension to help teach them a better way. So, if possible, step into that moment to have the conversation.

If you won't get the privacy and time you'll want in that moment, mention it to them or make a note to have this conversation when it's easier to talk. But you'll want to do this soon, certainly within a day of their slip.

When to Follow Up

Following up should happen frequently, beginning the very next day after having this conversation. That's the thing with this topic; many of our teenagers encounter it every single day, all day. You'll want to encourage them, and it's worth doing that sooner rather than later. When you follow up, you're wise if you find ways to share how you've been more intentional with your words as well. Your teenager will be more willing to follow your lead when they know you're working on this in your own life.

PREPARING THEM FOR THEIR FIRST JOB— WITH BETTER WORK HABITS

As parents, we prepare our teens to become responsible adults. Since our kids will spend decades working as adults, helping them develop good work habits makes sense.

Why This Is Important

Our work habits say something about us . . . good or bad. As Christians, we're ambassadors for Jesus. People should see Christ in us, especially in the way we work. Do we cut corners? Are we dependable, doing what we say we'll do? Do we need reminders to get our work done on time? Do we complain about the work or our coworkers?

Here are a few more reasons why developing better work habits matters.

- Having a reputation for being a good worker is priceless.

    A good name is more desirable than great riches;
    to be esteemed is better than silver or gold. (Prov. 22:1)

- Great pain awaits people with lazy work habits.

    The craving of a sluggard will be the death of him,
    because his hands refuse to work. (21:25)

- God isn't pleased with laziness. He equates it with being downright destructive.

    One who is slack in his work
    is brother to one who destroys. (18:9)

When we think about it, we can see the wisdom in that. Laziness is a misuse of the time, abilities, and opportunities God gives us.

Before tackling this topic with our teens, let's do a quick heart check. I've met tons of parents who don't want their teens working—not even with regular chores around the house. They want them to devote themselves to their studies. Or they insist their teens are too busy with all their super-important extracurricular activities. They make a valid point that these things lead to scholarships—which is sort of like earning money with a job. But unless teens get a *real* job, they won't gain important life experience like how to work for a tough boss, deal with annoying coworkers, and more. And unless they do work around the house, how are we preparing them to be independent?

Training our kids to be good workers at home—or as employees—is part of our job. It's best to do that while we still have a say in what they do, don't you think?

For starters, let's be sure our teens are doing a fair share of the work at home. And that means doing the tasks on time, without needing reminders, without complaining, and with excellence. Even something as small as being responsible for weekly tasks around the house helps prepare teens to be better employees or employers and better mates someday, for sure.

Assigning chores at home is needed, but we can try a different approach. Teens *don't* like being told what to do, but they *do* love to be independent. We can be smart and use these two facts to our advantage. Rather than assign "chores" at home, we can frame these tasks to our teens as "skills" they need to develop to be independent someday. If we present it this way, we'll potentially get less pushback.

- They'll need to learn how to do laundry, wash dishes, clean the house, cook, and do basic home maintenance and yard work.
- They'll need to learn how to do these things over long periods of time, so they develop the life skills of dependability and efficiency.

This really works. Think of driving, for example. Our teens need to learn how to drive. It's a life skill they'll need in order to be independent. Most teens don't complain about the hours they put in practicing driving. That effort paves the way for them to become more independent. The idea is that we approach chores around the house the same way.

Now, back to the topic of our kids doing better at work outside the home. We'll look at this in more detail in the "You Want Them to Get a Job" scenario, but right now, we're emphasizing the importance of our teens working.

My (Tim's) sons held jobs while in high school. It was *good* for them. Selfishly, my wife and I would've liked them home more. But the things they gained continue to pay valuable dividends.

When our sons went to college, we couldn't help them financially like we would've liked, and we didn't want them taking out loans. So, they began to work their way through college with the good habits they'd already been building.

And they did it. All three maintained solid grades. None of them came out of college with debt. And here's the big one: None of them got involved in a party lifestyle. They simply didn't have the time. They were working. I'd often felt bad that I couldn't help them more, but in the end, it was the best thing for them. The fact that they worked actually *protected* them.

Talk to your kids about work habits and be ready to get behind this. I honestly believe we'd see a lot fewer adult kids moving back home—or still living at home—if parents did a better job helping teens build solid work habits.

WHAT TO SAY

Rather than just jumping into this conversation, build some anticipation. Tell your teen that you want to share something with them that's an important key to leading a successful and satisfying life. Schedule a specific day and time to share a meal and talk it over. You might start out with something like this.

"There are so many things that are important to becoming independent and being a 'success' in life, and today I'd like to share a big one: Be an excellent worker.

What type of work habits would be typical for an excellent worker, would you say?"

Brainstorm a bit. Here's a list of prompts, if needed. See how many they can come up with and fill in as needed.

- Working hard and doing high-quality work.
- Being responsible by getting work done on time without needing reminders.
- Being dependable. If we say we're going to be at work, we're there—on time.
- Being honest.
- Working well with others.
- Maintaining a good attitude. Doing our work cheerfully, without complaining.

"Not many workers actually check all the boxes. If you do, though, you'll stand out in a good way. You'll build a great reputation—which is valuable."

Share Proverbs 22:1: "A good name is to be chosen rather than great riches, and favor is better than silver or gold" (ESV).

"In a world where more and more people are very anti-Christian, they'll have fewer stones to throw at you if you're a great worker/coworker. You'll be a good example of what a Christian actually is. That's pretty important.

On the other hand, if you're slow to get to work, to do what needs to be done, how might you hurt yourself—or the name of Christ?"

Give them a chance to come up with some answers on their own.

"The Bible warns that the lazy, slothful person hurts themselves." Share Proverbs 21:25 with them: "The desire of the sluggard kills him, for his hands refuse to labor" (ESV).

"As your parent, I want to encourage you to build strong work habits, whether it's on the job or in the home. Can you see how this will benefit you?"

If they're strong in one area of work habits, compliment them. And talk together about which ones may need work. Maybe pick one for starters, which will also make it easier when you follow up later. How do they build better work habits in that area? Brainstorm ideas with your teen, including where they'd need to start.

- Are they always late? Maybe they need to start using a calendar or start setting alarms on their phone so they're consistently building toward the habit of being fifteen minutes early.
- Do they never seem to have enough time to get their things done? Talk to them about how they might monitor their screen time.

Help them make a list so you can periodically go back and review it with your teen.

Alternate Way to Say This

Check out appendix A. The Let's Watch a Movie approach is effective. Can you think of a movie where someone distinguishes themselves with hard work? The Let Me Tell You a Story approach is also good here. Can you think of someone who has a powerful story of being a good or a bad worker? How did things work out for them? These stories provide examples to your teen of what to shoot for—or avoid. The story of Jonathan in 1 Samuel 14 is another example you can use. In his downtime, Jonathan could've hung around the camp like the rest of the army, but he wanted to see if God had more for him to do. What resulted was a massive victory against their Philistine enemies. Jonathan used his time to do something productive and became an undisputed hero as a result.

If you know a business owner, the Let's Take a Field Trip approach could also work really well. Set up an appointment to talk with that boss in person—along with your teen. If you ask them to tell your teen what makes a great worker, you won't have to.

When to Say This

There's no magic moment. You just need to make sure to have this conversation with your teen. If they're under sixteen years old, you're letting them know that you'll expect them to get a job—and what kind of worker you want them to be. In the meantime, you want to make it clear that good work habits start at home . . . with their chores.

When to Follow Up

If you pay your kids an allowance, or if they have a job, "payday" is a great time to circle back and talk to your kids about this. Make this a periodic conversation.

- How are you doing with your work habits?
- How are you distinguishing yourself as a great worker on the job?

If there were specific areas to work on or strategies they were going to try, this is when you'll want to go over that with them. Congratulate them on their successes, and help them fine-tune their strategies, if needed. You want to do everything you can to encourage them along.

YOU WANT THEM TO GET A JOB

Flipping burgers. Carrying golf clubs. Stocking shelves. First jobs aren't exactly glamorous. But the benefits of working? Undeniable. It's about so much more than earning extra spending money.

Why This Is Important

A job teaches teens something about their purpose and gives them important tools they'll need to become the man or woman God has called them to be.

- *God created work.* Genesis 2:15 says, "The LORD God took the man and put him in the Garden of Eden to work it and keep it." Considering how much people hate their jobs, you'd think God gave work as a consequence of sin! But actually, work came *first*. Work was part of the "good" God created. Working is embracing part of who God created us to be.
- *God works, and he gives all of us work.* Jobs to do. Responsibilities to oversee. It's part of being bearers of his image—and the work we do points to our Creator. Our teenagers are at a critical age to learn the "good" of work and the role it plays in God's purposes for their lives.
- *A job teaches our teenagers the value of self-discipline.* The Bible speaks highly of a good work ethic. Proverbs 6:6–8 says,

    > Go to the ant, O sluggard;
    >   consider her ways, and be wise.

> Without having any chief,
> > officer, or ruler,
> she prepares her bread in summer
> > and gathers her food in harvest. (ESV)

Those who are self-motivated to work are wise and prepared for the season ahead.

- *The Bible warns of the dangers of laziness.* Proverbs 20:4 says,

  > The sluggard does not plow in the autumn;
  > > he will seek at harvest and have nothing. (ESV)

  Laziness leaves one unprepared, empty-handed, and disrespected. Building a good work ethic happens over time, during those long shifts, as we put aside what we *wish* we were doing for the sake of what we *need* to be doing. There's no better time for teenagers to learn good work habits and the sacrifices necessary to build them.

- *When our teenagers work, it gives us the opportunity to teach them how to manage their money well.* Topics like budgeting, saving, and tithing can all be addressed, no matter how small their paycheck.

- *If they learn these important habits now, it will be easier for them to apply them later when they earn more and have more responsibilities.* We're preparing them to succeed.

WHAT TO SAY

"There are many exciting things ahead as you get older and become more independent. Getting a job is one of them. I think we're ready to talk about you starting to work soon." You want to build excitement for getting a first job. To do that, talk months in advance about working as something they *get* to do because they're older (like driving or having a later curfew).

This may end up being multiple conversations over the next months. In these mini-conversations, you can:

- *Have fun talking about options of where to work.* Talk about places that are fun for them to frequent now or where their personality would fit well. **"Wouldn't this be a cool first job? Let's remember this one when we start deciding where you'll apply."**
- *Emphasize the "good" of work.* **"When you begin working, you're experiencing something God created for us to do."**
- *Talk about a good work ethic and the kind of worker they want to be.* **"How can we start building those good work habits now?"** We listed some things in the previous scenario, "Preparing Them for Their First Job—with Better Work Habits."
- *Mention the benefits of work—like extra spending money, being trusted with more responsibility, and preparation for more independence.* These are things they want. It's important to make the connection: A job is how they arrive at their desired destination. **"This is going to be so good for you."**

When you're ready to talk about them actually getting a job, build some anticipation. **"I want us to start the process of finding you a job. I'll want to hear your ideas, and I'll bring my ideas as well. Let's find a time in the next week when we can talk through this."**

Here are some points to cover when you meet to talk.

"This is a really big step in growing into the man/woman that God has created you to be." You'll underscore the main points about what a job is and why it matters. You've already been running through these talking points with a bunch of mini-conversations; everything you've discussed these last months has set you up for this moment to drive the point home one more time.

"**Okay, let's talk through options.**" Help them decide which jobs to pursue. You might need to talk some sense into them if they're aiming too high or getting too picky. This is a great chance to remind them that there are benefits to almost all work, no matter the position or role. God's "good" in work applies even if we're flipping burgers or washing cars.

"**Here are your next steps.**" Help create a plan for everything they need to do for the application process. You don't want to pester them to "just go fill out that application!" Instead, come alongside them and teach them how to do it. It's helpful to set a deadline. Let them know when they should have all their applications turned in.

This is also a great time to talk to them about what is non-negotiable in any job. Do you want them to work on Sundays? If not, they'll need to note on the application that they're not available that day.

"**When you hear back from an employer, tell me so we can talk through what's next.**" Sometimes teenagers don't tell their parents they've heard back from an employer . . . for days. You want them to tell you so you can celebrate with them for every yes and help them process through every no. This also opens the door to talk about how to interview.

Alternate Way to Say This

Try the Field Trip approach in appendix A. Maybe take them to a place they're considering applying to. Or, better yet, take them to the location of *your* first job. Tell them stories from that job, and as you laugh together, they'll get excited for the experiences they're about to have at their first job.

When to Say This

Ideally, this is many conversations, spaced out over months. The main portion of the conversation isn't one you handle quickly or in passing. Find a spot where you can settle in and won't be interrupted.

In my (Mark's) personal opinion, this talk pairs well with a milkshake. This is a super-positive moment in their life. Get them excited! This talk should be fun, so embrace that with an environment to match.

When to Follow Up

Check in a week after their applications were submitted. They might've gotten rejections but were too embarrassed to tell you. A weekly check-in allows you to stay involved without being too overbearing.

Once they land the job, the check-ins continue for a couple of months but shift to asking your teenager about the job.

- "Is the job what you expected?"
- "What do you enjoy about it?"
- "What has been difficult?"
- "How are you getting along with your coworkers and your boss?"
- "How are you distinguishing yourself with a good attitude and good work habits?"
- "How have you been spending/budgeting the money you've been earning?"

YOU'RE SEEING PRIDE ISSUES

"I'm so proud of you!" How many times have we said that to our kids? Or maybe, "You should be proud of yourself." Parents tend to encourage their kids along with that kind of praise. And our kids definitely need to hear compliments and praise from us. But sometimes the way we praise our teens can contribute to them developing a pride issue.

A toddler looking back at us with a goofy, proud smile after taking their first wobbly steps? That's cute. But we see so many proud, arrogant adults in our world—and that's downright ugly. Somewhere along the line, we as parents need to help our teens strike a healthy balance.

Why This Is Important

Pride was the root behind the fall of Satan, tons of Bible characters, and countless people throughout history. Pride destroys the proud person—and the relationships they have with others. Life will be harder for our kids if they have pride issues. As James 4:6 says, "God opposes the proud but shows favor to the humble."

God *opposes* the proud. If our kids have a proud heart, God will work against them. That's an incredibly terrifying thought! We want God to bless our kids and help them navigate life. Let's help our teens with this pride thing, okay?

WHAT TO SAY

Keep this simple. **"Pride wears plenty of disguises. Can you list some attitudes or behaviors that really boil down to a pride issue?"**

Here's a list of prompts, if needed.

- bragging
- arrogance
- selfishness

- a sense that they're more important than others
- an air of privilege: "People should do things for me because I'm pretty special."
- failure to "see" others or their needs
- taking the best for oneself
- expecting others to serve them instead of serving others
- mocking or making fun of others; putting others down
- being unforgiving
- jealousy
- difficulty submitting to parents or other authority
- lack of respect for parents or others
- false humility (often to look good or to prompt others to praise them)

Your goal is to help your teen see that pride is ugly, dangerous, and wrong. Then you can talk about how to avoid pride.

"Sometimes I say, 'You should be proud of yourself,' or 'I'm so proud of you.'

The thing is, if you really took what I said to heart, I wouldn't be doing you any favors. You could become proud in a bad way. Who gives you your abilities and opportunities, along with the strength and health to do what you do?"

The obvious answer is God.

"God hates pride. Why do you think that is?"

Allow them to wrestle with the answer a bit. Here are some prompts and Scripture to help them as needed.

- Pride shows that a person has taken credit for the health, strength, abilities, opportunities, and smarts God has given them. That's stealing . . . *from God.*

> For who makes you different from anyone else? What do you have that you did not receive? And if you did receive it, why do you boast as though you did not? (1 Cor. 4:7)

> You may say to yourself, "My power and the strength of my hands have produced this wealth for me." But remember the Lord your God, for it is he who gives you the ability to produce wealth. (Deut. 8:17–18)

- Pride is putting oneself above others—considering oneself to be more important—something the Bible clearly teaches against.

   > Do nothing out of selfish ambition or vain conceit. Rather, in humility value others above yourselves, not looking to your own interests but each of you to the interests of the others. (Phil. 2:3–4)

   > God opposes the proud but shows favor to the humble. (James 4:6)

This would be a great time to explain that you'd never want God opposing them—and that they don't want that either.

"Often, we think that we just need to aim at being humble. The thing is, once we think we've hit the bull's eye, we've totally missed the target. So, how do we combat pride?"

Let them think for a moment, then move on to what may be the most effective way to have an attitude that's free from destructive pride: *being grateful*.

"Gratitude is the key. When we realize God gave us all our abilities and opportunities, along with the health and strength to do whatever it was that made us proud, our heart develops the right attitude. A grateful heart is the most effective way to combat pride, in my experience."

Once you've covered this ground with your teen, you can encourage them to ask God to show them their pride and help them develop a grateful attitude.

Alternate Way to Say This

This would be a great example of a conversation to move into the Object Lesson approach described in appendix A. If you picked up the books suggested, check out "Marshmallow Man" in *The Very Best, Hands-On, Kinda Dangerous Family Devotions*, vol. 3.

When to Say This

A great time to say this is after you've praised your teen about something they've said or done.

Otherwise, just have the conversation over dinner or a snack. You might even go online in advance to find an article or news story where someone is showing obvious pride. That opens a discussion about the harmful effects of pride and what to do about it.

Around the Thanksgiving table would be another great choice. Rather than the tired "What are you thankful for?" approach, you can mix it up a bit. Perhaps the question this year could be "If we aren't thanking God for things regularly, how might that indicate we have a pride problem?" or "How does expressing our sincere gratitude to God regularly keep us from the devastating effects of pride?"

When to Follow Up

The "when" here isn't as important as the fact that you do follow up. Once isn't enough. Make this a habit. Any time you praise your teen about something, lead them into expressing gratitude to God for the abilities, opportunities, health, and strength God blessed them with.

If you do this, you'll be helping your teen succeed in so many key ways. They'll be a better friend and perhaps a better mate to someone someday. They'll be a better worker too, I think. They'll have better relationships all around, and God will give them something we all desperately need in life. Grace. Favor. Remember, "God opposes the proud but shows favor to the humble" (James 4:6).

YOU'RE SEEING ANGER ISSUES

The ringer went off . . . *again!* Only ten minutes into the sermon, someone's phone had already gone off a handful of times. It was totally distracting to everyone within earshot. I (Mark) scanned the room, trying to find the rogue phone. How the owner of the phone ignored it was a complete mystery. A few seconds later it happened again. Another call! Somebody *really* wanted to get their attention.

This time I pinpointed the source. If he wasn't going to silence his notifications, I would go help him. I slipped out of my seat and tapped the man on the shoulder. It was obvious from the desperate look on his face that the poor guy had no idea how to turn off the ringer. His solution? Bury the phone in his pocket and sit there helplessly, hoping it wouldn't happen again. I asked for his phone, and he gratefully accepted the help.

Why This Is Important

Like that ringer on the phone, our teen's anger can disrupt their world—and everyone's around them. Ignoring the flare-ups does nothing but guarantee it'll happen again, to their own hurt and embarrassment. Stifling or silencing anger is only a temporary fix. Notifications on our phones tell us someone is trying to get through to us, and anger is a notification as well: It tells us there's something deep inside of us that needs our attention. Often our teens are like that man in the church service. They have no idea what to do when their anger rings—and deep down, they desperately want help.

Anger isn't always bad. It can be harnessed for good purposes when it comes from a good heart and right motives. Or it can be motivated by a sinful heart and be expressed in sinful ways. We want our teenagers to recognize the difference.

When is anger good? Every time we see God's anger, it's directed at sin. Therefore, when we get angry at sin, either in our lives or in the world, our hearts are like God's. David expresses this kind of anger in Psalm 10. When our teens feel anger like this, it'll actually help them live in obedience to God.

When is anger bad? Anger rooted in our personal sin—like selfishness, pride, jealousy, and greed— results in damaging, sinful actions toward others. Unrighteous anger leads us away from God and deeper into our own sin. Two verses to consider:

> Be angry and do not sin; do not let the sun go down on your anger. (Eph. 4:26 ESV)

> Refrain from anger and forsake wrath. Fret not yourself; it tends only to evil. (Ps. 37:8 ESV)

Our teens experience anger frequently. When that "notification" comes in, they need to assess if it is good anger or destructive, sinful anger—and deal with it properly. If they aren't able to discern between the two, they might end up trying to put the good anger on silent or let the bad anger continually ring and disrupt their lives.

Anger is a call to action. Let's help our teenagers understand what their anger is saying and what to do with that message!

WHAT TO SAY

Start casually. **"Let's compare who has more unread texts on our phone right now, you or me."** Have fun with it either way. If their number is high, you can joke about how popular they are. If it's low, they have their life in order!

"Our anger is a lot like text notifications. There's always a message behind it. Anger alerts us that something deeper in our heart needs our attention."

Provide an obvious example: Someone with road rage cuts another driver off. What does that anger reveal about their heart? Now transition to your teen. It'll be super helpful to give them a specific example of where you've seen their anger.

"As you think about your anger (a current situation or something in the recent past), **what message do you think it gave you about your heart?"** Look at their anger with them, as if you pulled out their phone and started reading through their texts.

"Sometimes anger can be right and good. Sometimes it's sin. The key to telling the difference is to look at the reason for our anger and how we express it. Are we angry with sin, or is our anger born out of sin—and causing us to sin? The Bible tells of times God got angry, but it wasn't wrong because God is never wrong. Sin angered God." Here's where you help your teen see what caused their anger and understand the message it reveals about their heart.

- *Good cause*: Wrong things in the world around them make them upset.
- *Bad cause*: Wrong things in their heart trigger their anger, like selfishness, pride, jealousy, or greed.

"It can be hard in the moment to know if our anger is good or bad because we often justify it. I think that's one more reason why we're told to be 'quick to listen, slow to speak and slow to become angry' in James 1:19. This kind of reaction gives us a chance to evaluate our heart, read the text, and better understand what we should do with that message."

How do we, as parents, personally do this? What are ways we slow ourselves down, especially in the middle of a meeting or while driving 70 mph down the highway? Anything we've experienced as helpful (or even the things that we know don't work), can be shared here as encouragement. Also, talk about how to channel good anger in good ways. By doing this, you'll give your teen tools to try the next time they feel angry.

"When you feel anger rising in you, think of it as a text buzzing in. You have to read it every time and figure out what's at the heart of your anger. No more unread anger. If your anger is good, you still need to channel it. If your anger is rooted in selfishness or pride, can you see how important it is to deal with your heart issue right away?"

Teens can be like that man in the church service, clueless about what to do next. You can help walk your teen through what they need to do when their anger is born out of sin:

- Confess to God.
- Ask God to change their heart.

Alternate Way to Say This

Try the Handoff approach in appendix A if you know a police officer who might share consequences they've seen as a result of people failing to control their anger (road rage, domestic violence).

If your teen's anger is rooted in deep emotional pain, consider the Ask the Expert approach and see a pastor or Christian counselor.

When to Say This

It's powerful to talk about this while your teen is still angry. You can help them process their anger and understand its root and how to handle it. Now, if things are too explosive in the moment, wait until they cool down—but not so long that their anger is past tense.

Be warned: If you talk about this while they're angry, they'll likely struggle to communicate well. They might say things that are unfair or illogical. This is all part of helping them learn to understand their anger. It requires extra effort on your part to stay patient and not be reactive. By the end of this, you might even find that you have some anger notifications you need to read as well!

When to Follow Up

There's something about the next morning, isn't there? Sometimes the freshness of a new day provides clarity we didn't have the day before. The heart is softer, like the morning light. Try talking to your teen before school.

Then, a bit later, send them a text: **"Are your text notifications on silent at school? I hope so! But remember, keep your anger notifications on, and keep reading those messages. Deal with them; don't bury them. Thanks for talking yesterday. I love you!"**

TEEN DISHONESTY

This week my (Mark's) son told me that he saw a fire truck flying in the sky. He was dead serious.

You think I believed him? Nope. It's pretty easy to tell when a two-year-old is lying. As he gets older, he'll have the same tendency to lie. But his lies will be more believable—and come with bigger consequences.

Why This Is Important

God's view of dishonesty is clear. Proverbs 6:16 says, "There are six things that the LORD hates, seven that are an abomination to him" (ESV). What makes the list of hated things? You guessed it: "a lying tongue" (v. 17). We should feel just as strongly about lying, even if our teenagers' lies feel small, isolated, or insignificant.

Lying has a way of devastating relationships. Paul talks about this in Ephesians 4:25.

> Therefore, having put away falsehood, let each one of you speak the truth with his neighbor, for we are members one of another. (ESV)

In other words: Don't lie, because when you do it messes with your closeness with others. We lose trust in a lying person. We lose unity too. If our teenagers are lying, they're hurting all their closest relationships.

Dishonesty is often the gateway to other sins. As we lie, we simultaneously sear our conscience and harden our heart to the truth. We cover up who we are and what we do, which allows our sin to go unchecked. The longer it sits there, the more comfortable we get with sin itself. At the root of our teenagers' greatest sin struggles is often some level of lying and cover-up.

When we address deception, we get at the foundation of ungodly living.

WHAT TO SAY

There are two goals for this conversation. First, that your teen would tell you the truth. Second, that they'd see the importance of not lying in the future.

For this scenario, imagine confronting them at the moment you believe they've lied to you.

"**(Name), are you lying to me? Are you being 100 percent truthful?**" They're probably ready to back up the individual details of their lie. But this question sidesteps that and gets to the bigger issue. This helps avoid their built-in impulse to continue the lie they started.

But here's my favorite part about this question: You've just named their sin. If they're lying, they're likely spinning a narrative in their head. They haven't thought about it as *lying* as much as they've focused on the benefit of not getting caught. They're justifying their dishonesty to protect themselves—or for some personal gain. But now you've called it what it is, and they can't escape the accurate label. And the 100 percent truthful part of your question is this: They see you're not asking them to be *mostly* truthful with you but *completely*. That puts them face-to-face with the fact that they're omitting or downplaying some details so that they look good.

"I want you to tell me the truth for a lot of reasons. But the biggest reason is because I know that being completely honest is what's best for you." They'll have their reasons why they weren't fully honest. You'll want to help them understand that telling the complete truth is more important than any reason to mask it.

Use the Scripture verses in the section above. If God hates lying, it can't be best for us. How can God bless us? When we lie, we destroy relationships. Make connections to their behavior and how some relationships might be impacted by their dishonesty. However, you don't want to get preachy with a lecture here.

When someone lies to us, it's deeply personal. As hurt and angry as you may be, this conversation must be done with a tone of love as you direct your teen toward truth. Yelling these truths at them will only push them to put up thicker walls of deception.

"I'm going to give you a chance to tell me what happened again, but this time with all the details—fully accurate. I know telling the truth goes against all the logic in your head right now. But remember, this is for your good." Say this in a kind, caring way, perhaps in a very quiet voice. When they verbalize the truth, it helps correct their impulse to say untrue things.

Right now, they lie as a reflex, mainly because it has massively benefited them in the past!

When they've lied in the past, they learned it helps them avoid some consequences of their behavior. This step of the conversation helps calibrate them toward telling the truth today and also for future situations.

"Is there anything else you left out?" Usually, the first telling of a story isn't the full edition. Let this question sit. It might feel a little awkward. That's okay. If they've hidden any part of the story, it's probably the hardest thing to say. It might take some silence on your part to draw it out.

"I'm really glad you told me the truth. This is an important step in the right direction. But there are still consequences to the lie you told." You want to make sure they see all the consequences. It could be something obvious, like, "Hey, I've lost trust with you in this area." Try to go one step further and show what that loss of trust changes or affects. "Hey, I've lost trust in you to be honest about how you and your friends spend your time. Therefore, I'm going to require you to be home earlier as we rebuild this trust over time."

One of the worst things you could do here is to rescue them from the consequences of their lying. That's one of the reasons they lied in the first place: to protect themselves. So, if you shield them from consequences, you haven't done much to discourage dishonesty in the future.

The memory of these consequences helps them make different decisions in the future. It's better to tell the truth even when we know it will hurt than to feel the pain of lies down the road.

"Over the next week, every time you talk or text, I want you to ask yourself 'Is this fully true?' God's expectation is complete truth, every time. God's standard must become our standard, no matter how big or small the situation."

Alternate Way to Say This

This would be a great opportunity to use the Let Me Tell You a Story approach in appendix A. Think of a time you saw a lie wreak havoc in your life, a friend's life, or maybe the life of a celebrity, pastor, or political figure. Your teenager will see how the consequences played out in real life without having to go through it themselves. This opens the door to talk with them about being honest—all the time.

When to Say This

It's best to have this conversation in the moment you suspect your teen is lying. If you miss that opportunity, follow up within a day. The longer you wait, the trickier it is to identify and uncover the actual truth.

You'll get the most honest response if you address this one-on-one, privately. With other people around, they'll feel the urge to say whatever is needed to keep up their front.

When to Follow Up

After a week, see what they've noticed when they ask themselves the question *Is this fully true?* as they speak or text. Notice you aren't asking "How's it been going telling the truth?" That's too vague and makes it easy for them to generalize so they look good.

CONCERNS ABOUT DEMONSTRATING GOOD LEADERSHIP

We might worry that our kids are living like followers instead of leaders. And maybe they're following the wrong people—or we fear they will. Let's talk about this with our teens in a way they might not expect.

Why This Is Important

Followers are vulnerable, right? They can be swayed by others and make bad decisions that hurt them over the long run. It's easy to think that the solution is for our kids to be better leaders. To think for themselves rather than follow someone else's lead. Often, we push our kids to be good leaders because we believe that's best for them.

But there's something missing with this approach, and it may be the very thing that helps our teens the most in this leadership scenario.

Rather than pushing our kids to be leaders, we should consider talking to them about becoming good *followers*. The Bible is filled with examples of good and bad leadership. The determining factor often came down to who the *leader* followed. People who followed ungodly advisers, the crowd, or their own desires tended to become poor leaders.

A babysitter is a leader. So is a crossing guard. Big brothers and sisters are leaders—even if they don't want to be. So, yes, we want our teens to learn to lead. But often our kids won't lead in the "big" ways we tend to think they will. The truth is, God didn't create all of us to be that type of leader, but he did wire us all to be followers.

> You must obey my laws and be careful to **follow** my decrees. I am the Lord your God. (Lev. 18:4, emphasis added)

> Whoever does not take up their cross and **follow** me is not worthy of me. (Matt. 10:38, emphasis added)

Some of the greatest leaders in the Bible are simply those who learned to follow God well. Moses. David. Peter. Paul.

Even the president of the United States must listen to the voters—or their party—and should follow the good examples of those who have sat in the Oval Office before them. A good president is a good follower.

The skill that is massively underdeveloped in our teens is being good followers, which starts with recognizing who is *worth* following.

WHAT TO SAY

Before getting into this conversation, do a quick Amazon search of how many books are listed with the word *leadership* in the title, and use that number as you open this conversation.

"Did you know that Amazon lists over 57,000 book titles with the word *leadership* in the title? Why do you think there are so many books available on the topic?"

Any answer they give works. Just take it from there.

"Sometimes I think parents focus too much on pushing their kids to be leaders. There have definitely been times I've wanted you to step up to be more of a leader. I've wanted you to make better decisions rather than let others think for you. But I think I was missing something important, and I want to fix that."

That tiny admission at the end is the key to this conversation. That will make your teen more willing to listen. It isn't every day Mom or Dad admits they've gotten something wrong. But if you've ever put more emphasis on being a good leader than being a wise follower, you can honestly say you were a bit off the bubble.

"More important than being a good leader is being a good follower. What do you think I mean by that?"

Use whatever they say as your ramp to the next question.

"God wired us to be followers:

- **To follow him and his Word.**
- **To follow his Son. Jesus proclaimed, over and over, 'Follow me.'**

- To follow the examples of those who have wisely lived for our Lord.

The Bible instructs us to be good followers much more than it reminds us to be good leaders. Our culture often has this upside down, don't you think?"

You want to be sure they're tracking with you. A nod of the head is enough.

"All leaders follow somebody. They have someone they answer to, such as a boss, voters, or stockholders. Or maybe they follow a family or a historical hero. They follow someone. The best leaders are really followers who know *who* best to follow.

The Bible gives plenty of examples of leadership, but the outstanding leaders were those who followed God closely. What can we learn from that?"

Give them a chance to verbalize what they're thinking. You might ask who they think is worth following and who isn't. Talk about the fact that sometimes we can follow people in one area of their life but not in others. When we follow any human being 100 percent, we're headed for trouble.

"With all the talk about the need to be a better leader, hopefully this takes a little pressure off you. You just need to make wise choices about who to follow and do it well."

This is where the conversation can get uncomfortable for your teen, especially if they think you're about to rag on them for the friends they follow. Instead, lead off with some personal examples from your past of how you followed someone's example, advice, or demands . . . and how that proved to be a costly mistake. Once you've done that, you're ready to move on. "We have to ask ourselves these questions every now and then:

- Am I following Jesus like I should? How can I do that better?
- Am I following some people who aren't following hard after God? If so, what should I do about that?"

> You've taken this conversation to a really good spot. Be careful not to preach at them now. Think of this as a coaching session with your teen. You want to help them succeed in life—and you've just given them a huge tip toward doing that.

Alternate Way to Say This

Check out the Game approach in appendix A. Make a game of listing people who it would be wise to follow in some aspect of their life—and those it wouldn't. **"I think following _____ with how they're so kind to others would be wise. But to take their example on handling money? Well, that wouldn't be so smart."**

Once you've played the game, it opens things up for a conversation about leading and following.

When to Say This

The idea of being a good follower and choosing wisely when it comes to who we follow is a pretty grown-up topic. So, treat your teen like a young adult when you hit this topic. Take them out to dinner—maybe even this Saturday night.

In truth, almost any time will do. But Saturday night is good because the following morning they'll be at church, surrounded by people who might make good candidates for following.

When to Follow Up

Revisit this topic about two weeks after your conversation. Take the opportunity to ask how they're doing with the issue of making wise "following" choices.

- Do they have any examples of how they've made changes or adjustments?

- What about you? Do you have examples you can give them of your leadership/following choices in the last couple weeks? This will go a long way toward reinforcing these principles.

If anything has come up in the meantime, such as an example of a really good or bad choice somebody made as a leader or follower, you can use that as a great way to make what you've shared about leading/following come alive for them.

12

THEIR EMOTIONS

YOUR TEEN SEEMS TO BE DEPRESSED

The thought of our kids becoming depressed is one of those dreaded parental fears. Tragically, in today's culture, it's more common than ever before. Depression is as insidious as a demon and just as dangerous.

If you're reading this page, you've already seen something in your teen that is troubling. And if you've seen something, please, please, please follow through—quickly.

Why This Is Important

So many teens attempt or succeed with suicide, often for reasons their parents could have massively helped them with, had they known. Tragically, those teens chose a permanent course of action to deal with a temporary problem.

Sometimes the enemy deceives teens into thinking suicide is the only solution. The brave solution. The last thing they want is for their parents to talk them out of suicide, so they hide the signs. Terrifying, right? Which underscores the importance of having this conversation *now*.

Other times our teens may not go so far as to consider suicide, but they live in a continual emotional storm of depression. They may cut themselves where they're sure you won't see it. They suffer silently. There are so many other things that they may do . . . none of them good. Teens can also normalize this depressed condition, often because they see it in friends. Depression may be *common*, but it isn't *normal*. We want our teens to experience life out from under that cloud of depression.

WHAT TO SAY

You don't want to be at all vague with this conversation.

"I've noticed you don't seem quite yourself. You seem more (down/withdrawn/depressed/whatever you're noticing). Something is haunting you. Talk to me."

If they ask you what you mean, you can explain as much as you think they need. But if you suspect they're acting naive to throw you off the trail or to put the ball back in your court, chest-pass it right back—and *fast*. You can't let them sidetrack you. Remember, this is a matter of life and death. If our enemy has deceived them, he'll try desperately to end this conversation or move it in a different direction.

You might say something like **"I think you know what I mean. What is it?"** or **"I'm your parent. I just know. So, talk to me. Tell me everything. What started things?"**

If your teen opens up, your tendency as their parent will be to "fix" things—which may not be enough for them at their stage. Other times parents tend to tell their teens what *they* need to do. But if your teen is at some level of depression, their capacity to "do" has massively decreased. Solutions that require your teen to take some kind of action, no matter how small, may seem like ascending Mt. Everest to them. Even worse, your teen will feel like you're piling more things on them, which can push them closer to the edge.

- You have to walk them through, making sure they're fully on board with the course of action.
- You have to take them by the hand and help them through the next steps to climb out of this depression. This may necessitate the help of a professional Christian counselor. You need to get on this—*today*.

No parent wants to think their teen has considered suicide. But the most effective way to protect them may be to get that out in the open.

"I think a huge percentage of teens have considered suicide at some point, even if it was just a fleeting thought. What about you?" This is a huge question—and very deliberately worded. By starting with the fact that many teens have considered suicide, you make it easier for them to be honest with you. From here, depending on their answers, their body language, a nudge from the Holy Spirit, or your parental gut feeling, you'll want to dig deeper with other questions.

"Have you ever attempted suicide?"

"Do you have a plan for how you would commit suicide if you ever felt you had no other choice?"

If they have a plan currently or have made any suicide attempts, you'll want to take them to the ER immediately and get them professional help.

You've asked your teen to be honest with you. Be honest with them. Have you ever considered—or attempted—suicide? It might be good to let your teen know how grateful you are that you didn't follow through or weren't successful.

If you're convinced your teen isn't suicidal, you need to end this conversation by moving right into the next steps you've just talked over with them to help your teen climb out of this depression. It won't get better by itself.

Alternate Way to Say This

In appendix A, you'll see an option called the Ask the Expert approach. A depressed teen is not an issue you can delegate, but you may need some expert help. I would absolutely get a solid Christian counselor involved right up front.

When to Say This

Today. Tomorrow at the latest. The point is, think of depression as a burning building. The longer you wait to help pull your teen out, the more deadly it becomes.

One thing to consider is the time of day. Normally, you'll want to be able to watch your teen during this conversation. What they say. How they say it. Their body language. If they are suicidal—and intent on hiding it—you'll need every advantage you can get. So, this suggests having the conversation during the day, when you can see them clearly.

On the other hand, daytime can be the hardest time to get really open answers from our teens. Remember, sometimes they don't like looking us in the eyes, not for long, anyway. They don't enjoy feeling like they're being studied. Put your finger on this page to bookmark it, and quickly flip back to chapter 1, "Prepping for the Talk with Your Teen." Find the heading "Atmosphere Is Important." You'll do yourself a huge favor by giving the suggestions there a quick read before having this talk with your teen.

Personally, I (Tim) think I'd have this conversation at night, sitting around a fire pit, or on the edge of their bed, relying on the Holy Spirit to show me what I can't see and to help me discern where they're really at.

When to Follow Up

Constantly. Daily. Depression is a shadow monster. It can hide, then suddenly reappear. Once that door of communication has been opened, keep it that way. Have frequent talks on the topic. One honest talk rarely fixes everything. Consider this an ongoing conversation you'll need to have.

A few more thoughts. First, there's an interesting verse in Proverbs that gives us another thing to think about.

> Like one who takes away a garment on a cold day,
> or like vinegar poured on a wound,
> is one who sings songs to a heavy heart. (Prov. 25:20)

Someone who takes away our coat on a cold day isn't helping us. If we don't find shelter, we'll die of hypothermia. And sometimes the music we listen to when we're depressed isn't doing us any favors. When we're down, we might like the songs that show we aren't alone. But according to Proverbs, this won't help. It only makes our situation worse. It accelerates the ill effects. Let's keep that in mind with our teens when they're struggling with depression or massive discouragement. What kind of music are they playing? What kind of music *should* we have playing in our homes? I wonder how many teens were emboldened to attempt suicide over the years after listening to Blue Oyster Cult's "Don't Fear the Reaper" (1976), even though many argue the song had nothing to do with taking one's life.

I think the same principle applies to the movies we watch. Right now, if you have a teen battling depression-like issues, it will be wise to surround them with uplifting music and movies. You'll want to avoid anything that romanticizes death, especially that of someone who is in some kind of emotional crisis.

Second, we want to trust our teens, but we must always verify that what they say is true. I've seen it too many times. Teens wrestling with suicidal thoughts often hide them from their parents.

They display the kind of behavior we want to see, and we believe they're getting better. They want to keep us from probing—and from stopping them. So, even if your teen assures you that suicide never was or will be an option, keep your eyes open.

Last thing: Remember the dad who brought his demon-possessed son to Jesus in Matthew 17:14–20? The demon somehow caused the boy to fall into water or fire. The demon was *trying* to cause the boy to commit suicide. But this dad knelt before Jesus, begging for his help. And this dad brought his son to Jesus. He didn't *send* his boy to Jesus. He *brought* him. There's a lesson or two in there for us, don't you think? Let's kneel before Jesus, my friend. He is merciful, and right now, with a depressed teen . . . his mercy is exactly what you need. Do everything you can to bring that son or daughter you love to the feet of Jesus too. Like the man in this biblical account, as parents, we should not let our teens out of our sight until Jesus has set them free.

YOUR TEEN SEEMS CONSUMED WITH ANXIETY

You're waiting for those test results; the doctor should've called by now.

You're sitting in traffic and already late.

Your company has been hit with massive layoffs, and you wonder if you're next.

Something is off with your relationship with someone you love, and you don't know how to fix it.

Your teen has applied to all the colleges on their list, and now all you can do is wait to see which ones say yes.

Anxiety. Can you feel it? You probably have at some point this week. Maybe even right now. It hits in so many areas of our lives, playing on our fears and worries of the unknown. Often, it's something we silently struggle through. It can be so hard to talk about anxiety and even more difficult to overcome! Our teens wrestle with anxiety, too, and they need our help.

Why This Is Important

Our culture talks a lot about anxiety these days, and our teenagers are listening. What they need is less of what our culture is selling—and a whole lot more of what the Bible teaches.

Often our culture says anxiety is too powerful to control. We talk a lot about managing anxiety and not as much about working through it. Teens often have a sense of helplessness about their condition that fuels even more anxious thoughts.

Anxiety has become a normalized by-product of living in our fast-paced, highly productive society. And the term *anxiety* can be used for everything from worry to an actual diagnosed disorder. In this scenario, we are primarily talking about the former. The world is telling our teenagers:

- They need to control their future by putting in the hard work now—which will naturally cause some anxiety.
- If they aren't anxious about what's ahead, they're not working hard enough or dreaming big enough. In other words, if they're not feeling a bit anxious, there's something wrong with them.

Some in our culture view this kind of anxiety as a badge of honor to validate one's efforts. If you're anxious, welcome to the club; we all are! We have a way of celebrating anxiety as we passively accept the fact that accomplishing the greatest things in life will require the gut-wrenching pain of worry.

But the Bible teaches another way.

- When we accept what the world says about considering a certain level of personal anxiety as being okay or even

desirable, we contradict God's command in Philippians 4:6: "Do not be anxious about anything, but in every situation, by prayer and petition, with thanksgiving, present your requests to God." As if disobeying the command not to worry isn't enough, we also forfeit the opportunity to grow deeper roots of trust in God.
- Every moment of worry or anxiety is an opportunity to deepen our understanding of God's character. His power compared to our limitations. His sovereignty and control of the future. His faithfulness for provision. Everything changes in this world, but God never does.

Let us be clear: Serious anxiety disorders are real. If you suspect your teen's anxiety may be at a diagnosable level, don't delay seeking professional help.

For situations where anxiety is not a potential mental health disorder, it's still dangerous—and something we need to deal with. This type of anxiety is not just a feeling to ignore or bury or a crippling experience to suffer through. Anxiety and worry can be a *strength exercise*. When we handle our anxiety according to what the Bible teaches, we grow stronger in God. In our weakness, we're made strong. Here's what the Bible says about handling worry and anxiety:

- Jesus says, "Come to me, all you who are weary and burdened, and I will give you rest" (Matt. 11:28).
- "Cast all your anxiety on [God] because he cares for you" (1 Pet. 5:7).
- Peace is found in God, and his peace "will guard your hearts and your minds in Christ Jesus" (Phil. 4:7).
- In God's goodness, he'll lead us, protect us, and provide us with all we need (Ps. 23).

- "Can any one of you by worrying add a single hour to your life?" (Matt. 6:27). We shouldn't passively accept anxiety but instead trust God with the details of our life (6:25–34).

WHAT TO SAY

Your teenager probably won't approach you, asking to talk about their anxiety. It's a hard topic for them to bring up on their own, especially if the stuff they're worried about is super personal. What's more usual is that you'll need to initiate this conversation as you see signs of anxiety in their life. Be on the lookout for indecisiveness, restlessness, stress, fatigue, increased irritability, trouble sleeping, nail biting, more screen time, or more time alone in their room.

Bring up the topic in a gentle and caring way.

"I've noticed you're more stressed lately. Can we talk about it?" Gently bring up some of what you're seeing. As you do, you're giving them an opportunity to talk about it. It's a win here if they talk at all about what they're feeling. As they talk, listen for what is at the heart of their anxiety. It's going to involve a desire for control at the very foundation, but be on the lookout for themes: school, friends, career, or personal insecurities.

"You aren't alone. Many people struggle with worry and anxiety. It's something I've struggled with in my life big-time." Even though this information is not earth-shattering, this is an important moment. You aren't bringing this up to normalize anxiety like pop culture does. You're doing this to establish some good examples for how to deal with it.

It will also help in making them feel more comfortable to share. The more vulnerable you are with sharing your anxiety struggles, the more likely they are to open up. Resist the temptation to give them solutions for worrying or to talk about victories you've had in this area. That will come in a little bit, but hold tight on that for now.

"Let's think together. What are the things we feel anxious about during the day?" This is a bit of a callback to your first question, but you're hoping your teenager is a bit more open to talking about what's really there, especially after you've opened up. Maybe they give other examples or just go into more detail about what they've already shared with you. You can dig deeper with some good follow-up questions here, like

- "How long have you felt that way?"
- "Wow, how did you handle that?"
- "Did you ever talk to anyone else about how you were feeling?"

"I'm sure you've seen stuff on social media or heard friends talk about their anxiety. What do you think about their methods for handling anxiety?" There might be some things here that are helpful, and that's fine to affirm them. But hopefully, as you expand a bit on this part of the conversation, you can highlight how the way the world approaches anxiety and worry falls short.

So often people focus on methods used to *control* their emotions—which result from the *lack of control* in their life. It's just a cycle that highlights the problem. Oh, and the solution their "managing tactics" offers? It's us! The world is selling *self-help*, as if we can somehow attain deep peace in our own strength and ability to control our life. Now we're *really* stressed! The world's way won't ever work, because it puts us in the place of God as the one in control.

"When we're anxious, we want to control something we weren't meant to, and we worry about something we don't have to." You can spend some time here, showing how our anxious feelings go back to an element of desiring control and lack of trust for the future. Be specific with the examples you both shared. And as you do, you can share the Scripture verses noted earlier in this scenario. Many times, our teens experience temporary anxiety that is performance-based—like just before a game, a play, or a test. We can help them handle that kind of anxiety much better than they are apt to do.

"Let me tell you what it has looked like for me to trust God with the plan for my life." You've already shared vulnerably about how you've struggled, and that gives you a platform to speak about what has helped you. Try to be specific about what it looks like to trust God with your future.

- Is there anything you've stopped doing?
- Have you started any habits to help your heart trust God?

This could be a great spot to look at Matthew 6:25–34 and what Jesus taught us to do when we're anxious: Look at the birds!

"Let's commit for the next thirty days to pray about our anxiety. Let's spend time every day asking God to help us trust his plan and his way." One of the best parts about praying this every day is that it highlights our lack of control and power and emphasizes our dependency on God—who is in total control and has infinite power. It gets right at the heart of our worry.

You'll join your teen in this challenge for lots of reasons, but mostly because it will help you to have better follow-up conversations if you have real examples to give.

Note: Our teens can be good at hiding symptoms—or putting up a facade that suggests they're doing better than they really are. They may have trouble sleeping, have stomachaches, or be losing weight. They may be irritable, have trouble concentrating, or have personality changes. They may even have a sense of impending doom or hopelessness or suicidal thoughts they aren't telling you about. Unless you're absolutely certain their anxiety isn't approaching a dangerous level, please see a professional counselor as suggested in the next section below.

Alternate Way to Say This

You might try the Field Trip approach in appendix A. The further you can get away from it all with your teen, the better! Sometimes physical distance from the things stressing us out can help us process them easier. If you try this, you'll want to both commit to keeping your phones off. Your teen's phone will probably bring reminders of the very things stressing them.

Another alternative would be the Ask the Expert approach. Even if you don't believe your son or daughter could have a diagnosable anxiety disorder, getting a professional Christian counselor involved may be the wisest course of action. If your teen isn't responding to your attempts to help or doesn't seem to be making measurable improvements, bring in a professional. This isn't something to dare using a "wait and see if this works itself out on its own" approach. Get a professional Christian counselor involved sooner, not later.

When to Say This

If you can carve out a thirty-minute time slot right before bed, you'll set yourself up for a great environment for this conversation. Your teen is lying in bed, their phone is away, the lighting is soft, and things are comfortable. It's in that moment you can address the things eating away at them. Their anxiety is such a stark contrast to their surroundings.

When to Follow Up

Follow up the very next day. You've agreed to pray together about your anxiety for the next thirty days. Why not mention something the very next day about that prayer time you've already had? It will encourage them to hear that you're following through and push them to do the same.

Here's a handful of helpful verses you might want to share with your teen.

> Truly my soul finds rest in God;
> > my salvation comes from him.
> Truly he is my rock and my salvation;
> > he is my fortress, I will never be shaken. (Ps. 62:1–2)

> Cast your cares on the LORD
> > and he will sustain you;
> he will never let
> > the righteous be shaken. (Ps. 55:22)

Depending on the severity of their anxiety, you might need regular check-ins and follow-ups. Also, once again: There are definitely cases in which anxiety requires counseling from a Christian professional. It's important you get them the help they need—fast!

YOUR TEEN'S SELF-WORTH SEEMS AT AN UNHEALTHY LOW

There are times we may feel that something's off with our teens' sense of self-worth. We need to trust our gut and pay attention—because it's really important.

Maybe a teen lacks drive. They're sleeping more than they should. Or maybe they spend too much time doomscrolling on their phone or escaping into some video game. They're not talking much about friends or out doing things with them. It may even seem like they're isolating themselves.

Maybe our teens seem to have a hard time looking us in the eyes, and when they do, we're not seeing much excitement about life there.

Our teens may make negative comments about themselves, especially in comparison to others. They measure their worth based on what they see in others. Often it is about appearance or popularity. Other times it's about abilities. "I could never do that," they say. Or they may do more of the opposite, bragging about their own accomplishments and tearing down others.

They may resist branching out to do or try new things, and we suspect that deep down they fear they can't—or they don't want to face another failure. They may overreact in bad ways to criticism and discount any praise we give them. We may find their grades are suffering and they're making poor decisions—or can't seem to make a decision. Maybe our teens don't appear to have dreams about their future that truly excite them.

Teens with low self-esteem may react in a wide variety of ways. But rarely will they work harder to change their sense of personal value in ways that are good and healthy.

Often, as parents, when we feel our teens have a sense of self-worth that is too low, our tendency is to build our teens up. We might overly praise their accomplishments to them and to others, especially family. It's as if we're hoping others in the family will praise them, too, and somehow our teens' self-image will rise to a healthy level. This generally is a very temporary fix—if it works at all.

Another tactic we use is to tell our teens how much we love them. While that's a really important thing to do, it rarely raises self-esteem. *Of course Mom/Dad loves me*, they think. Any decent parent loves their kid, right?

Let's take a closer look at how we can help them.

Why This Is Important

Low self-esteem rarely leads to anything good. When our teens truly believe their value is lower than it should be, they're vulnerable.

- They are vulnerable to others who want to use/manipulate them for their own selfish desires.
- They are vulnerable to the enemy who wants to destroy our teens and keep them from ever accomplishing the plans God has for them.

To be protected, our teens need much more than for us to praise them or build them up somehow. At the root of low self-value is simply having a wrong view of themselves. What they need is to understand God's perspective of who they are. Then they can build a healthy self-esteem or self-worth.

WHAT TO SAY

Point them to God right off the bat.

"Most people grow up thinking they're a product of their mom and dad. And there's some truth there, but it goes deeper than that. Who actually created you?"

Give them some Scripture to make this clear:

> For you created my inmost being;
> you knit me together in my mother's womb.
> I praise you because I am fearfully and wonderfully made;
> your works are wonderful,
> I know that full well.
> My frame was not hidden from you
> when I was made in the secret place,
> when I was woven together in the depths of the earth.

> Your eyes saw my unformed body;
>> all the days ordained for me were written in your book
>> before one of them came to be. (Ps. 139:13–16)

For we are God's handiwork, created in Christ Jesus to do good works, which God prepared in advance for us to do. (Eph. 2:10)

"According to these verses,

- God created you.
- God has a plan for your life. He's created you to do some really good things that you're likely totally unaware of.

How should that make you feel?"

They may not be feeling much of anything right now. But as the truth sinks in, it has the power to change hearts.

"What kinds of things might God have planned for you?"

Though we can't know for sure, as adults we've lived long enough to see some of how God's plans have worked for others. Brainstorm some basic things with your teen to give them hope.

- Very few people were created to win Olympic gold medals. But often God creates encouragers . . . people who help others stay on the right paths and make good choices.
- God creates influencers: people who lead a life that's attractive and points the way for others to begin a relationship with God.
- A good friend is valuable and rare, and God creates people who will be able to be that kind of friend.
- God creates us to be loving, self-controlled, patient, strong, and kind—things that don't come naturally to

people. God gifts us with all these attributes in supernatural ways, with the help of his Holy Spirit, to accomplish his purposes.

Likely God has things planned for us that we can't see or guess, but they're *good*. We have God's Word on that, and sometimes we need to trust him to reveal those things at the right time.

"Often, we measure our self-worth by comparing ourselves to others. How have you seen that—or maybe even done it yourself?" Usually it's about physical abilities, appearance, and so forth. "But God's designs for us are so much deeper than that. We are God's masterpiece. Unique. Made for his special plans. Do you see how we can get sidetracked by comparing ourselves to others?

Does our enemy know God created us—and that he has a plan for us?" For sure. The devil and his demons know what the Bible says, and they believe it too.

"Sometimes I think our enemy looks for ways to make us view ourselves with much less value than we really have in God's eyes. He's hoping we never become the people God designed us to be or experience the joys God intends us to have. Does that make sense?

How can we fight back—and have a proper view of ourselves—so we can continue with that plan God has for us?"

You're looking to get a bit of discussion or brainstorming going here. You might want to take notes as you do, so together you and your teen can form a strategy moving forward. But the foundation is that your teen isn't simply the end product of a biological act. They were created by Almighty God for his purposes. That should spark something deep inside your teen, such as hope that there's much more to their life than they may have thought or that is apparent at this point.

Alternate Way to Say This

This might be a good case for the Ask the Expert approach in appendix A. If you sense the need for a Christian counselor or psychologist, do it. Another alternate might be the Object Lesson approach, specifically "Messy but Valuable" in *The Very Best, Hands-On, Kinda Dangerous Family Devotions*, vol. 1.

When to Say This

Even if your teen doesn't seem to be struggling with self-esteem issues, this is still an essential talk to schedule. But if they *are* wrestling, you'll want to have this conversation in the next few days. Self-esteem issues don't necessarily stay constant, at one level. Teens can continue to slowly spiral deeper into their dark place, making them harder and harder to reach.

Take some time to prepare and pray.

Finding a place out in nature to have this talk with your teen can help. Do you live by mountains? A lake or stream? How about going out when there's a beautiful sunset? It makes a good place to remind them that God creates great things in nature—and in us.

When to Follow Up

Issues of emotional health are critical, so you'll want to follow up soon. That means within a few days, not weeks. If you don't feel your conversation has made the needed difference, you must act on that immediately. You can't expect that this situation will just get better on its own. Get professional help from a Christian counselor or psychologist.

13

THEIR PERSONAL VIEWS AND CONFORMING TO CULTURE

> **YOUR TEEN IS DEVELOPING VIEWS THAT NO LONGER AGREE WITH SCRIPTURE**

Roughly half the adults in the United States wear glasses. That's more than 149 million of us who need help seeing clearly. If our teens needed prescription lenses, we'd be all over that. Without glasses, they'd struggle with depth perception, reading, and a world out of focus.

God's Word works like glasses, helping us and our teens see our world clearly. Our hearts and sinful desires distort how we see life. On our own, we'll adopt perspectives that aren't right and fumble our way through life. If we want clear vision for our teens, we need to help them view the world through the lens of what the Bible says to be true.

Why This Is Important

Teenagers often begin to see the world from perspectives differing from Scripture. They'll be tempted to make decisions based on what seems best for them, even if it contradicts what the Bible teaches. That never ends well, and we don't want that for our teens.

In the book of Judges, we read how the people of Israel had no king ruling over them, and they weren't acknowledging God's authority over them either. "Everyone did what was right in his own eyes" (21:25 ESV). They knew what God expected from them but chose instead what seemed best from *their* perspective. They chose sin and suffered terribly as a result.

When we—or our teens—simply do what is right in our own eyes, it often leads us away from God and what's good for us. It's dangerous to walk through this world with our own hearts and perspectives guiding us!

WHAT TO SAY

Have some fun with this conversation. Find some cheap glasses (at a thrift store or pharmacy) that have super strong magnification. The stronger, the better!

Now ask your teen to do some tasks while wearing those glasses. Nothing too dangerous such as driving or riding a bike. More like reading aloud, doing some chores, shooting hoops, threading a needle, playing a video game, or applying makeup. As long as the glasses distort enough, they'll struggle and mess up. Perfect!

"How tough was that to do while wearing those glasses?" Relive the experience of watching them struggle from your perspective. Laugh about it together.

"Imagine doing something more dangerous while your vision was distorted. Can you think of things that might be bad?" Driving. Riding a bike. They might suggest some absolutely crazy things to do while wearing the glasses. Play out all those what-ifs; it's moving this conversation in the right direction.

"It's dangerous to trust our vision when we wear these glasses. In life, we see everything through a different set of glasses. Our opinions, perspectives, experiences, desires . . . all that and more create the lenses through which we see life and make decisions. If our 'lenses' are off or distorted, how might that prove dangerous to us?" Give them a moment to think on that. Can you share a bad decision you made because you saw a situation only from your perspective—which turned out to be distorted?

"Our vision of what is right and wrong is often blurry because our perspective of what is true and good is distorted. We make bad decisions when we trust our own way of seeing the world. Where can we go—what book can we turn to for a right and clear focus on every aspect of life?" God's Word, of course. Read Proverbs 3:5–8 (ESV) together then talk through these key phrases:

- "Do not lean on your own understanding." In other words, don't rely on your own view of things. You won't lead yourself anywhere good on your own.
- "In all your ways acknowledge him, and he will make straight your paths." Let God set your course. View the world from the perspective of what he says is right and good.
- "Be not wise in your own eyes." This goes back to the danger of trusting our lenses instead of the true lens of Scripture.
- "It will be healing to your flesh and refreshment to your bones." There are so many benefits to viewing the world through the truth of God's Word.

It would be awesome to share an example from your life when you thought you saw something clearly, but God's Word convicted you and put you back on the right path.

"When we trust our own way of seeing the world instead of God's way, we'll run into obstacles and dangers we could've avoided." Get specific. If you see your teen trusting their own perspective instead of God's Word, talk about the consequences of that blurry vision.

"We want to use the lens of what the Bible says to be true to see the world, including our friendships. School. Family. Career. Politics. Current events. Struggles. Our passions. What's right and wrong." *Doing* this isn't as easy as simply putting on a pair of glasses. It takes some effort and a working knowledge of what the Bible actually says. They might not know yet how to look at everything in their life from a biblical perspective, but at least they know that's their goal. That's a great start.

> All Scripture is breathed out by God and profitable for teaching, for reproof, for correction, and for training in righteousness, that the man of God may be complete, equipped for every good work. (2 Tim. 3:16–17 ESV)

God's Word has the 20/20 vision needed to teach, correct, rebuke, and train us. His Word is truth and helps us see a path forward clearly—for our ultimate good! What does this say about our need to be in the Word daily?

Alternate Way to Say This

Take your teen somewhere you can get total darkness, such as your basement or your church at night. If it's a familiar place to them, set up a few unexpected obstacles and have them wear sunglasses too. Ask them to navigate their way through the dark room.

They'll struggle, bump into things, and might even stop walking at some point. Perfect.

Now have them do it again, with a flashlight. Much easier—because they see clearly. Connect that to Psalm 119:105: "Your word is a lamp to my feet and a light to my path" (ESV). In life, they'll have times they think they know best. But if they're walking according to their own perspective instead of God's truth, they're walking in the dark when they could be using a flashlight!

When to Say This

It'll take a little planning ahead to have the distorting glasses ready to go. Once you do, create a good opportunity for your teen to wear them—like when they're about to start chores. They might like the idea of having a little game with the glasses instead of getting right down to work.

When to Follow Up

This whole topic should become regularly random. There are infinite opportunities to see if your teen is wearing *their* glasses or looking through the lens of Scripture. Make this a reflex action on your part; look for ways to talk about the biblical perspective as you watch shows, read news stories, or observe life experiences (yours, theirs, or their friends'). Make a family habit of asking how you should view every situation and decision through the lens of what God says.

HELPING YOUR TEEN NAVIGATE TRUTH ABOUT IDENTITY AND GENDER

Be honest, did you skip to this chapter first? I (Mark) get it; this topic piques interest. It's the center of cultural debate, yet we cringe at the idea of our teens having questions about this.

As parents, many of us would much rather sit this one out and let the youth pastor handle it. Or we just hope someone else helps our teenagers through this one—or that they miraculously adopt the truth on their own. There's plenty of reasons we might be tempted to avoid this discussion.

- Even though we'd be sharing truth, this topic is awkward and hard.
- This issue has the potential to put a barrier between us and our kids.
- The stakes are so high. If our teens don't embrace a biblical view, they'll end up confused, vulnerable, and unable to help their friends find the truth.

But all these reasons for avoiding this discussion are the same reasons we need have it.

Why This Is Important

Someone will shape how our teenagers think about this topic, *but most sources will not give them the truth*. Anytime our teens believe lies, they're in danger. Our teens absorb information and opinions daily from social media, friends, teachers, shows, movies, podcasts, music, advertisements, celebrities, and political leaders. Here's what our teens hear:

- Everyone can choose their own identity and gender.
- Gender isn't necessarily determined at birth. We can choose our gender based on how we identify, see, or *want* to see ourselves.
- Gender is fluid. We have the right to change our gender at will.
- Changing one's gender identity is a show of strength, a brave step toward finding deep inner satisfaction and fulfillment that can be found no other way.

- Embracing these views of gender fluidity is a mark of wisdom and enlightenment.
- To oppose or question anyone's choice of gender is more than just unloving, it is an act of hate. Anyone attempting to talk someone out of a gender change—even a parent—is being hateful.
- We must actively support and celebrate people's gender, identity, and name/pronoun choices. Indifference or silence is opposition.
- We can't assume someone's gender based on their name, bodily appearance, clothing, or the sound of their voice.

By the way, it's very possible this list will become outdated . . . tomorrow. Because that's how some of this works. The narrative is evolving as the pressure for "gender inclusion" grows.

Some Christians roll their eyes at this whole topic. Those who take a dismissive approach tend to alienate the very ones they so desperately need to reach. So, before even getting into this conversation with our teens, let's do a personal heart check. When we talk with our teens, we want our tone and body language to reflect our love for them—and for those who are caught up in the confusion that has gripped our world.

Our teens are getting very mixed messages from friends and adults they respect, even from many vocal and convincing Christians. Our enemy, the devil, has done a masterful job of deceiving so many on this topic, and those who disagree are labeled as "haters." If our teens are struggling with what is really true and right, a cavalier or condescending attitude on our end will absolutely push them away from us. If we make sarcastic remarks about those who advocate gender fluidity, *we* will look like a hater—and we'll be playing right into the enemy's hands.

So, let's show compassion to our teens and to those who are confused or spreading confusion about gender issues. Remember what 1 Corinthians 13:1 says: "If I speak in the tongues of men or of angels, but do not have love, I am only a resounding gong or a clanging cymbal." We can have the facts, the truth, and share it in a skilled way, but if we aren't speaking with love, all our teens will hear is *noise*.

And remember, to effectively protect our teens, listening only to what Christians who share our viewpoint are saying may not be enough. Likely there are people our teens respect who are giving them a different point of view. We need to be prepared for that. If we listen to how the world pitches approval for gender fluidity and learn to understand why people are lining up to follow along, we'll be that much better prepared to help our teens—but only if we do it in a loving way.

Here's some truth from God's Word that we need to hold on to as we look at what the world is saying about gender.

- God, as our Creator, is the only one who assigns gender. To say otherwise challenges his sovereignty (Gen. 1; Ps. 139:13).
- Our identity and purpose are established by God. He made us in his image, and we have purpose in the new life he has given us. *We view ourselves* based solely on how *he views us* (Eph. 2:10).
- Jesus is love, yet he constantly opposed sinful lifestyles. We can love others and stand opposed to their sin at the same time (Rom. 5:8).
- Our convictions of right and wrong come from God's unchanging Word, not the changing moral compass of culture (Ps. 119:105).
- God created male and female . . . just two genders (Gen. 1:27). Remember, God's Word trumps any past or present cultural definition of gender roles. Our culture is not more enlightened than God on the topic.

- This gender and identity revolution is a result of sin . . . humankind's rejection of God and his truth. It is an exchange of God's truth for lies and another example of how people who claim to be wise have become fools (1 Cor. 1:18–31).

WHAT TO SAY

This conversation is aimed at two things:

1. *Strengthen your teen's understanding of truth.* It's more common now than ever for teenagers to question the Bible's message on this topic.
2. *Help your teen to know how to relate to those with opposing views.* They're told it's unloving if they don't accept other people's lifestyle choices. Help them understand the difference between *acceptance* and *approval*.

"I know you hear stuff about gender. What's your take on whether it's right or wrong to identify as a different gender than our biological gender at birth?" You're acknowledging that there are different viewpoints out there and that you need to know where your teen is at. You might not like what you hear, but just make a mental note of that. You'll come back to it. Right now, you listen so you know how to direct the conversation.

If their answer comes from a biblical viewpoint, great! But don't end the conversation. Continue to strengthen their beliefs and their ability to share those with others.

"God created us. All his creation has purpose and is good." This is a great spot to check out some verses so they see where you're getting this.

- Genesis 1:27–29 hits on us being made in God's image. That image-bearing part is huge. Basically, God made us different from all creation—to represent what he is

like. We don't get to just change that without going against the way he set things in motion. His creation was good and has purpose. God doesn't make mistakes, not even with gender.
- Ephesians 2:1–10 talks about identity and purpose. As believers, Jesus Christ has changed our identity already. We were dead. Lost. Now we're alive. Saved. There is no other identity change that's needed—or that God approves. God has great plans and purposes for us. Good things he's created us to do and become through Jesus.

"If God is King of all creation, and he made us for his purposes, what would it take for us to change or overrule his purposes for us?" Only a new king could overturn God's plans. If we buy into the philosophy that it's fine to create our own identity and chase our own purpose in opposition to what God has decreed, then, in essence, we are in rebellion. We are rejecting God's authority and putting ourselves on the throne.

"To reject God's purposes in order to live out our own desires is sin." It's important to label gender transitioning and fluidity as sin. Remember, this may be completely contrary to what your teen has been hearing and seeing on their phone and at school. Go slow here, and do not make assumptions.

"Our purpose is to live out who God created us to be." This is where we spend our lifetime, aimed right here:

- We do the things God has called us to do and become the person he's planned us to be.
- We live out the identity God has given us, including our roles as son, daughter, brother, sister, husband, wife, student, employee, and so forth.

Living this out in our God-given and purposed gender is where we find contentment and joy in life.

"Sometimes people will say it's unloving for us to have these beliefs about gender and identity. Are you worried about that?" Let them share, and feel free to talk about ways you've felt pressure too. Be careful not to discount their concerns here.

"God is the definition of love. And his love doesn't let people choose their own self-destructive ways. He always calls us out of our sin and into obedience to God's way."

First John 4:7–12 is a nice passage to show God is love. This truth is so important to cling to as the world tries to redefine love.

"How do we react to people who don't share the Bible's views? Like Jesus accepted us when we were still sinners, we can accept others. That doesn't mean we approve of their sin. It just means we meet them where they're at and love them as Jesus loved us before we came to Christ." John 3:16 is helpful here. God, in his love, came to earth to save us. But don't miss how Jesus did that. He didn't say, "You live your truth and purpose and follow me." No, he came to give us new life. To put the old ways to death. We're to become more and more like Jesus.

So, the same goes for how we treat people who are in sin and far from God.

- We meet them where they're at in a way that shows Christ's love.
- We call them to new life in Jesus—the only one who can save our souls.
- If they take that step, then the Holy Spirit goes to work in them, putting their sin to death and changing them so they enjoy God's good purposes and plan for their life.

"Helping people see their need for Jesus is not unloving. The opposite is true. To simply 'accept' people where they are and leave it at that, knowing they're lost? THAT would be unloving." This mirrors the love of Jesus when he saved us. Jesus *accepts* unbelievers by meeting us where we're at in the midst of all our sin. But Jesus never *approves* of sin—or says it's okay for us to continue living that way if we want to follow him. He always calls us to faith and repentance, which will lead to us aligning our life and purpose with who God has created us to be.

"What questions do you have about this?" Chances are, something didn't stick or make sense. Give them an opportunity to double back.

Alternate Way to Say This

Consider the Let's Watch a Movie approach as described in appendix A. The movie doesn't necessarily need to have a character who has redefined their gender, but any movie that teaches the mantra "live your truth" would be a great bridge into this fuller conversation.

Another idea to ramp up to the bigger discussion is to go to the library and pick up the classic children's folktale *The Emperor's New Clothes*, by Hans Christian Andersen. In the story, we see how social pressure suppresses the truth. Sound familiar? It took a brave person to call the emperor's new outfit for what it was . . . a total illusion.

When to Say This

This is one of those talks that just needs to happen, even if you think your teen is solid in what they believe. Anytime is a good time. But if you want to be more strategic, here are a few ideas.

- June is gay pride month. Your teen will be seeing and hearing more about this whole topic. It would be a great time to talk through what you believe.

- Why not a little back-to-school theology prep? Right before a new school year is a great time; you know they'll hear and see a lot of different perspectives at school.
- The next time you see a show or movie with a character or message that contradicts the Bible, talk it through. It won't take very long for this to happen!

When to Follow Up

I know you'll be relieved when this conversation is over. But don't get too comfortable. Your teenager will need to talk about this again. And again. And again. Follow up after a week. Remember, current American culture is saying a lot about this, every day.

APPENDIX A

STRATEGIES TO MAKE IT EASIER FOR TEENS TO ACCEPT WHAT YOU'RE SAYING

Sometimes we have something hard to say to our teens . . . or we have to repeat something we've already told them a million times. My dad used to say, "There's more than one way to skin a cat." Now, I (Tim) don't know a thing about skinning a cat, or why anyone would want to. But the thing is, there's definitely more than one way to say something. Experiment. Get creative. Ask God to give you some different approaches that might bring better results.

Here are examples of twelve alternate ways to communicate something important to your teen, besides the straightforward conversation modeled in most of the preceding scenarios. Having a variety of approaches in your toolbox is a really good thing. Sometimes a different strategy can make all the difference.

Some of these are simply good options. Some can be silly. But all of them—used at the right time and in the right way—can be really, really effective. Are you ready? Here we go.

1. The **Game/Challenge** approach: Remember, back when your kids were young, how you got them to do things they really didn't want to do? Often you made a game of it.

- "Let's see how fast we can pick up the toys together."
- "If you finish the last three bites on your plate before Mommy cleans off her plate, you'll get something special for dessert."

How can you turn the thing you need your teen to do (like clean their room) into a game instead of a lecture followed by a chore?

2. The **Let's Go to Fantasyland** approach: This one is fun and extremely effective. Say your teen wants something—or wants to do something—that just isn't going to fly with you. Rather than firing off your list of logical, practical reasons why their idea won't work, join them on the journey. "Oh, honey . . . wouldn't that be great? If only we could send you to that $1,000 camp for the week. And not just you. What if we had the money so you could invite two of your friends too? Who would you bring?"

You're not fighting your teen. You're agreeing with them. They're seeing how you'd like that too. Usually, it becomes obvious to them why whatever it is that they want won't work.

3. The **Let's Brainstorm Creative Alternates** approach: Many times, the thing your teen wants—or the way they want a problem handled—is out of the question. You can pick their solution apart because the flaws in their plan are massive. That puts your teen on the defensive right away. It's like they are at one end of a negotiating table, and you're sitting at the other. Each side will

be trying to gain the advantage or get the upper hand over the other.

A better approach? Join them at their end of the table. "I'm not sure if what you're asking can work, but let's not give up on this. Let's do some brainstorming. When we put our heads together, I'm sure we'll find a good alternative."

Here's a ridiculous example of how this might work.

Teen: "I really want a giant honeybee tattooed on my forehead, but I'm underage and need a parent's permission slip."

Parent: "That's an interesting idea. Tell me why you want it so badly."

Teen: "I want others to see that I'm unique. Not afraid to try new things. And maybe that I'm as sweet as honey—but if they cross me, I'll sting them good."

Parent: "I *love* the messages you want to send. Let's brainstorm a bit and come up with a whole list of ways we can communicate those. Like a custom-made T-shirt or sticker for your water bottle, or . . ."

Can you see how a brainstorming session will keep you on the same side—and help you end up with a solution you both can live with?

4. The **Object Lesson** approach: Sometimes a powerfully effective alternate method to get through to teens may be to use an object lesson. You can use things like tomatoes, fire, rattraps, and more to get through to your kids in ways they'll never forget.

With that in mind, Tim has written three volumes of object lessons often referred to in the previous scenarios. If you have the books on hand right up front, you'll be much better prepared for when you need them.

Yes, doing so means spending more money . . . but it's well worth it if it helps some important conversations with your teen go well.

> Tim Shoemaker, *The Very Best, Hands-On, Kinda Dangerous Family Devotions: 52 Activities Your Kids Will Never Forget*, vol. 1 (Revell, 2019) ISBN 978-0-8007-3555-5
>
> Tim Shoemaker, *The Very Best, Hands-On, Kinda Dangerous Family Devotions: 52 Activities Your Kids Will Never Forget*, vol. 2 (Revell, 2023) ISBN 978-0-8007-4212-6
>
> Tim Shoemaker, *The Very Best, Hands-On, Kinda Dangerous Family Devotions: 52 Activities Your Kids Will Never Forget*, vol. 3 (Revell, 2024) ISBN 978-0-8007-4490-8

You can buy all three for under $40. Expensive? No. Valuable? YES.

5. The **Field Trip** approach: This is about taking your teen someplace to illustrate a point in a more visual way. You want to make a point that a movie illustrates perfectly? Take them to a movie. Is the talk about dating? A field trip to a used car lot will be something they'll never forget. This is one of those approaches that takes more time than a simple talk, but it can be much, much more effective.

Oh, and those three volumes of *The Very Best, Hands-On, Kinda Dangerous Family Devotions*? You'll be using them here too. Get the books.

6. The **No Free Lunch** approach: Often, parents do so much for our kids that they grow to expect us—and others—to *keep* doing for them. This approach provides a way of showing your teen that with privilege comes responsibility. Or that when they ask for a favor, they'd better be willing to give a favor right back. "You want to borrow my car—and I need you to give me some

time this week for something I want to talk to you about. So . . . got any ideas of how we might work this out?"

7. The **Shameless Bribe** approach: *Bribe* is a nasty word, so let's put it this way. There are times you can offer an *incentive* to your teen. You started doing this when they were little, didn't you? "One more bite—and then Daddy will get you some dessert." I (Tim) grew up in a home where Mom and Dad rewarded good grades on our school report cards. Sometimes offering an incentive isn't a bad thing. I'm not talking about a desperate, "Hail Mary" pass kind of thing but offering a reasonable reward. "If you can get your bedroom cleaned up before your friends arrive, I'll order pizza for all of you, just as a snack." Now, that doesn't sound so bad, does it? It sure beats the approach that says, "Get this room cleaned up, or you can text your friends and tell them not to bother coming."

8. The **Handoff** approach: This is not something you'll use often, but when needed, it can gain you some serious yardage with your teen. There are some topics or issues that will come up—and the honest truth? You're not the best one to talk with your teen about it.

- Maybe your relationship isn't strong enough right now to tackle this issue.
- Maybe you really don't have the answer.
- Maybe the topic hits an emotional PTSD button in you that makes this too hard to talk about.
- Maybe your teen doesn't respect you enough for you to talk to them about this issue.
- Maybe you don't have enough experience with the issue and know you can't help your teen as much as they'll need. Or maybe there's someone your teen respects who is better qualified to talk with them about the situation.

Whatever the reason, the end goal is that your teen would come around to a healthy, biblical way of thinking without rebelling. If the talk is more likely to go well with someone else leading it, the Handoff approach may be the best option in the playbook for this situation.

Maybe your spouse is the better choice. Or Grandma. Grandpa. An uncle or aunt. An older sister or brother. A mentor. Their youth pastor. It could be someone across the country—and your teen will set up a video call with them. Maybe this other person has experience in this area that applies perfectly to your teen's situation. Maybe they're so respected by your teen that your son or daughter will be readier to listen to this other person. Sometimes, as parents, we have to swallow our pride and realize that some topics or issues are just too important to leave solely to us. When it comes to this topic, you're second string—and you need a starter on the line.

If this is the approach you believe may be most effective, you may ask your teen if they'd be willing to talk to that particular person about the situation instead of just talking to you. Ideally, you join them when they talk to that person. But sometimes that might not be productive. Based on the issue and who you're handing it off to, you'll know if it's best for you to be around or not.

Once they've agreed to the handoff, you'll talk to that person to give them the background situation. You'll also want to be sure you're on the same page with the coaching they'll likely give your teen.

Years ago, when I (Tim) was in a critical conversation with my son, the coauthor of this book, I used the Handoff approach. I didn't want to. I wanted to be the one to help him. But I knew someone else who could do it better. That handoff was a tremendous, life-changing success. This works, my friend!

One tiny thought here: Sometimes we can combine the approaches. Perhaps you might use the Handoff approach, but while your teen likes the idea of talking to someone else, they don't like the person you're suggesting. Okay, now you employ the Let's Brainstorm Creative Alternates approach to come up with a name of someone both of you respect and appreciate.

9. The **Mysterious Letter** approach: This is one you'll use only on rare occasions. But if you only use it once—and it helps—you'll be flying high. Here's how it works.

Let's say your teen begged for a puppy a few years back. And you bought their line about how dedicated they'd be at taking care of the pet. But lately it's been *you* walking the dog—and the routine is getting old. You've suggested and hinted and asked them to walk the dog—but you're afraid the poor thing will have an accident in the house before they grab the leash. So, you handwrite a letter to your teen—from the dog—and deliver it or have someone else deliver it.

> *Dear Lily,*
> *Grab the leash and meet me at the door in two minutes. I've got something I want to show you outside. Lots of love and tail-wagging, from your favorite dog in the whole world!*
>
> *—Fluffy*

You know your kid. That kind of letter may work for your teen. Or maybe they'll need something a little less warm and fuzzy.

> *Hey Caleb,*
> *Grab the leash and meet me at the door in two minutes. I've got a nasty little surprise I'd like to leave on the neighbor's lawn. You've got to see this!*
>
> *—Bear*

10. The **Ask the Expert** approach: This is for those times when you're over your head—as in feeling totally unqualified to handle the situation your teen is in. If your teen is dangerously depressed

or facing great anxiety, your counsel may seem trite to them. If your teen is caught up in some kind of addiction or gripped in the talons of pornography, you may need expert or professional help. Talk to your pastor or youth pastor to get a referral for a Christian counselor in your area. You might also call Focus on the Family in Colorado Springs or visit their website. They have all kinds of resources and suggestions to help you with your next steps.

11. The **Let Me Tell You a Story** approach: Can you think of a story you heard or an experience from your own life that might perfectly illustrate some truth you want to convey to your teen? The story approach can be a great option. Want an example of someone who used this—with life-changing results? Read the account of when the prophet Nathan confronted King David in 2 Samuel 12. As a result of Nathan's story, David wrote Psalm 51. Take a peek at that to see how deeply a story can impact someone's life.

12. The **Let's Watch a Movie** approach: Basically, this is the same idea as above, but sometimes there is a movie, or a scene in a movie, that helps illustrate the issue you want to talk about. Watching it opens the door for discussion afterward. "You know, I keep thinking about how this one part of the movie illustrates an important truth for life."

Even a good novel can work if its underlying theme touches on the truth your teen needs. Sometimes there's no more powerful way to convey truth than through fiction! Read it to your teen or make it something you both read and talk about when you're done.

APPENDIX B

WATCH YOUR STEP FAMILY ACTIVITY

> THEME: The role of parents is to guide and protect their kids. Parents aren't trying to cramp your style... they're trying to keep you from becoming crippled.

THINGS YOU'LL NEED

- ☐ Rattraps, available at any hardware store. You're looking for the traditional type. Wood base. Nasty spring-loaded kill bar. They look just like mousetraps, only bigger. I picked up a pack of Victor brand traps, and they work great. One trap is enough to teach the lesson, but having more traps might help you make your point better. If you buy enough traps to give each of the kids one after the lesson, they'll have a nice reminder of what you taught them.
- ☐ Blindfold, or a scarf works fine.
- ☐ Wood pencils... only if you want to demonstrate the traps.

Advance Prep

After you've purchased the rattrap, get familiar with it a bit. Later, when you're with the kids, you'll want to demonstrate the power of the rattrap. There are a couple of potential ways to do that.

1. Hold the trap in one hand, pull back the spring-loaded kill bar a couple of inches, and, *making sure no fingers are in the way*, let it snap closed. It makes a nice, loud bang. This is an effective way to demonstrate the power of the rattrap to the kids.
2. The other way is to actually set—*and trip*—the trap. Set the trap on the floor. Carefully pull back the kill bar all the way. Then hold the kill bar in place with the tripping mechanism. Once the trap is set, take a pencil and deliberately press the bait pad to trip the release mechanism. The key is to hold the pencil firmly in place against the bait pad. As long as you don't let the pencil get brushed out of the way, the kill bar should slam into the pencil with enough force to snap it in two. After you've chosen and practiced which method you'd like to use, you're ready to do this with the kids.

Running the Activity

You'll want to start out by showing the kids the rattrap—and demonstrating its power in whichever way you feel most comfortable. If you're going to snap the pencil, I'd suggest you have the trap all set before they get in the room rather than trying to do it with the kids pressing in to see. Whether you snap the trap or snap the pencil, they'll get a feel for how much that trap would hurt if they stepped in it. If you have multiple traps, you can set the traps up in a maze across the floor. If not, just talk them through it.

Watch Your Step Family Activity

- Imagine I had each of you take off your shoes and socks and had a whole maze of rattraps set up across the floor.
- What if I asked for one of you to volunteer . . . and I blindfolded you (actually blindfold one of the kids), spun you around a few times, and had you march—not shuffle—right through that maze of traps?
- Very soon you would hear this (snap a trap in your hand like you practiced), and you'd be in a world of pain, right?

Now, if I really *did* ask for one of you to volunteer to go barefoot and blindfolded into that maze of traps—you wouldn't do it, would you? Nobody wants their toes in one of these traps.

- But what if we did it a little differently?
- What if you were still barefoot and blindfolded, but I had you face me and put your hands on my shoulders—and I put mine on yours?
- What if I carefully led you through the maze? Would you be more inclined to go through it then?

You might be a little scared, but if you really trusted me, you could be sure I would get you through that maze without you getting caught in any traps.

This whole rattrap activity is a picture of life. There are traps out there in our world. Nasty ones that can hurt you. Can you think of any?

- Drugs
- Alcohol
- Friends who aren't a good influence
- Smartphones used unwisely
- Too much time playing computer games
- Skipping time reading your Bible

- Wrong attitudes
- Pornography
- Choosing to live a secret life—hiding sin instead of dealing with it

The devil and his demons have all kinds of traps out there—just hoping you'll step in one. And if you do, you'll be in a lot of pain. The pain may be delayed—like the pain of regret. But pain always follows after sin.

But God doesn't want you to step in traps. He doesn't want you to hurt yourself—and others—like you will if you step in a trap.

That's one reason he gives you a mom. That's one reason he gives you a dad.

- A parent's job is to provide for their kids.
- A parent's job is to prepare their kids for the future—especially spiritually.
- A parent's job is to protect their kids—both now and for the future.

As you get older, the danger and intensity of the traps increase too. But God doesn't want you to go through these years all by yourself. That is one reason he has me here. I'm to guide you through the maze of traps.

So, sometimes I'm going to say no to things you really want to do. I'm not trying to be mean. I'm trying to protect you from traps that you might not see. I'm trying to do the job God gave me to do . . . and with God's help, I want to do it the best I possibly can.

If you think I'm being unfair, talk to me. And try to understand that sometimes I may still have to say no so that I provide, prepare, and protect you the way I believe God wants me to.

Here are some Scripture verses that help express my heart on this.

> In the paths of the wicked are snares and pitfalls,
> > but those who would preserve their life stay far from them. (Prov. 22:5)

I love you like crazy, and my desire is that I help keep you away from the paths where there are traps. Your life could depend on this.

> Hold on to instruction, do not let it go;
> > guard it well, for it is your life.
> Do not set foot on the path of the wicked
> > or walk in the way of evildoers.
> Avoid it, do not travel on it;
> > turn from it and go on your way. (4:13–15)

As a parent, this is my prayer. That you'll take what I've taught you—and that I'll continue to teach—and hold on to it. Guard it. Live by it. And avoid the paths that lead to doing wrong things. Those paths are loaded with traps.

> Don't let anyone look down on you because you are young, but set an example for the believers in speech, in conduct, in love, in faith and in purity. (1 Tim. 4:12)

First Timothy 4:12 is another prayer I have for you. Not just that you'll avoid the traps—and let me help you do that—but that you'll be an example of what a follower of Christ should be in the way you love others, in the way you talk, in the things you choose to do, in the way you choose to live a pure life, and in the way you trust God.

Summing It Up

Sometimes you hear these verses from the Bible quoted . . . reminding you about how you're to obey your parents.

> Children, obey your parents in the Lord, for this is right. "Honor your father and mother"—which is the first commandment with a promise—"so that it may go well with you and that you may enjoy long life on the earth." (Eph. 6:1–3)

I never want to use a verse like this in a negative way. It is a positive thing. Sure, it can be really hard to obey parents at times—especially when we say no to something you really want to do.

But this verse is a reminder to hang in there. To trust God with this—and to trust your parents. And if you honor and obey your parents, I can guarantee you're going to avoid some really nasty traps out there. That alone will be one way that things will "go well with you," as the verse promises. You'll avoid the pain and regret of stepping into traps.

Will you do that? Trust God . . . trust me . . . and we'll both help you avoid some traps—and make your life a lot better in the process.

"Watch Your Step" is an excerpt from Tim Shoemaker, *The Very Best, Hands-On, Kinda Dangerous Family Devotions: 52 Activities Your Kids Will Never Forget*, vol. 1 (Revell 2019). Used by permission.

APPENDIX C

EASY TARGET FAMILY ACTIVITY

> THEME: Going to church helps us stay on fire for Christ... avoiding church makes our passion easier to extinguish.

THINGS YOU'LL NEED

- ☐ Squirt gun / water pistol for each of the kids. You're *not* looking for a high-powered, super-soaker type. In this case, something smaller is better.
- ☐ Fire pit or campfire—and everything that goes with that. Logs, starting fluid, and matches or a lighter. You'll want at least one log to be smaller, maybe the size of your wrist.
- ☐ Fireplace poker, tongs, or fireproof gloves—really anything that will allow you to remove one small log from the fire.
- ☐ Stopwatch (such as the one on your smartphone).

Advance Prep

If you have the chance to practice this in advance, great. Running through it one time will make the activity go smoother when you do it with the kids. And it will also ensure that you have the right squirt guns for the job. You don't want ones that will douse the fire too quickly—or ones that will take forever to extinguish it either.

Your goal is to show the kids that a log in a fire pit or campfire is a lot harder to extinguish than one that is separated from the others.

Running the Activity

After your fire is strong and blazing, you're ready to begin the lesson.

- Separate one log—about the size of your wrist—from the fire pit or campfire.
- Give each of your kids a squirt gun and, using the stopwatch, time how long it takes them to extinguish that log you pulled from the fire. When they're done, there should be no visible flames on that log. It may still be smoking—and that's fine.
- Now put that log back in the fire with the rest of the logs and let it fully reignite while you refill the squirt guns.
- Ask the kids to extinguish the same log again—but this time while it's in the fire with the other logs. Allow them only the same amount of time they had when they extinguished it the first time (if you are using your phone, set the timer to the exact number of seconds it took to extinguish the log the first time).
- When the time is up, the kids must stop squirting.

As long as the squirt guns you're using aren't too big, it's unlikely your kids will be able to extinguish the flame while the log is with all the other burning ones. That's exactly the result you're looking for.

Teaching the Lesson

When the log was separated from the others, it was easy to extinguish. After the log was returned to the fire and reignited, its fire was much more difficult to put out, right? We did this to illustrate an important truth about Christians and the church today.

Sometimes when someone is really serious about their faith—about obeying God's Word, following his ways, and loving God—we might refer to them as being "on fire."

- Do you think that a Christian who is "on fire" is one who becomes a target of the devil and his demons?
- Do you think they seek to extinguish that Christian's burning desire to follow God?
- Do you suppose it would be easier to quench that Christian's dedication to God if that Christian were off on their own somewhere—or in a church surrounded by other solid believers?
- Because of school, sports, work, or just life, sometimes Christians don't make it to church every week. There has been a growing trend of redefining "regular" church attendance as being something less than it traditionally used to be. Sometimes a person who claims to be a regular church attender may go to church only once or twice a month. How might that make them an easier target for the enemy?

Listen to this verse:

And let us consider how we may spur one another on toward love and good deeds, not giving up meeting together, as some are in the habit of doing, but encouraging one another—and all the more as you see the Day approaching. (Heb. 10:24–25)

When this verse talks about the "Day," it is referring to a day in the future—when Jesus comes back.

- Are we closer to Jesus's return today than we were last year?
- What does the verse say? The closer and closer we get to that day, are we to be dedicated to getting to church with other believers more and more—or less and less?
- Why do you think God emphasizes in his Word that we need to be more dedicated to getting to church and being with other believers the closer we get to Jesus coming back?
- What does that suggest about some of the activities and things that keep us from getting to church?

Summing It Up

The closer we get to Jesus's return, likely the more intense the efforts will be on the part of the devil and his demons to extinguish our dedication to God. The devil and his demons are running out of time—and they know it. So, it only makes sense that they're dialing up their efforts to keep us from church and from burning strong for God. If our burning desire to live for God weakens, we'll be the ones who suffer.

And if we're not in church, we won't be there to urge one another on to love others and to do good. We won't be there to encourage others.

Going to church weekly and being surrounded by other believers is a really good way to help keep our flame burning strong—and for us to help others keep burning strong as well. It is no wonder that God wants us to get to church—to be with other believers more and more as the enemy steps up efforts to extinguish our flame. As we saw with the fire and squirt guns, we're a much easier target when we're separated from other believers.

Sometimes the less we get together with other believers for the purpose of strengthening our walk with the Lord, the more our relationship with God begins to cool. And often the sense of urgency to be with other believers cools down too. Let's do all we can to keep that from happening to us. Let's do all we can to follow God's Word—and stay burning for God in the process.

"Easy Target" is an excerpt from Tim Shoemaker, *The Very Best, Hands-On, Kinda Dangerous Family Devotions: 52 Activities Your Kids Will Never Forget*, vol. 1 (Revell, 2019). Used by permission.

TIM SHOEMAKER is the author of more than twenty books and is a popular speaker at conferences and schools around the country. He is a regular contributor to Focus on the Family *Clubhouse* and *Clubhouse Jr.* magazines. Tim loves writing contemporary novels for youth filled with mystery, adventure, and suspense, such as the award-winning *Easy Target*, *Escape from the Everglades*, and the rest of the High Water series. His contemporary suspense novel *Code of Silence* was named in the "Top Ten Crime Novels for Youth" by *Booklist*. Happily married for more than forty years, Tim lives in Illinois and still loves working with youth.

MARK SHOEMAKER is a Moody Bible Institute and Seminary graduate, has served as an adjunct professor, and has been a youth and family pastor since 2011. Happily married for over fifteen years, Mark is a campus pastor and oversees youth and college ministries at The Bridge Community Church in Illinois.

A Note from the Publisher

Dear Reader,

Thank you for selecting a Revell book! We're so happy to be part of your life through this work.

Revell's mission is to publish books that offer hope and help for meeting life's challenges, and that bring comfort and inspiration. We know that the right words at the right time can make all the difference; it is our goal with every title to provide just the words you need.

We believe in building lasting relationships with readers, and we'd love to get to know you better. If you have any feedback, questions, or just want to chat about your experience reading this book, please email us directly at publisher@revellbooks.com. Your insights are incredibly important to us, and it would be our pleasure to hear how we can better serve you.

We look forward to hearing from you and having the chance to enhance your experience with Revell Books.

The Publishing Team at Revell Books
A Division of Baker Publishing Group
publisher@revellbooks.com

www.ingramcontent.com/pod-product-compliance
Lightning Source LLC
Chambersburg PA
CBHW032224080426
42735CB00008B/704